Live High on Life™

For Teens

12 Simple Ways to Make the Most of Your Teenage Years

Becca Wertheim

Outskirts Press, Inc.
Denver, Colorado

Outskirts Press, Inc.
http://www.outskirtspress.com

ISBN: 978-1-4327-5803-5

Outskirts Press and the "OP" logo are trademarks belonging to Outskirts Press, Inc.

PRINTED IN THE UNITED STATES OF AMERICA

For my incredible family—especially my parents—and my amazing friends. Thank you for encouraging me to follow my dreams!

Table of Contents

The Live High on Life™ Style

4 Million Minutes

From the time you start middle school—for most people that's 6th grade—to the time you graduate high school, seven years will have passed. That's about 2,555 days, or 61, 320 hours, or 3,679,200 minutes! So think about that—nearly 4 million minutes make up our teenage years. That's a lot! A whole lot! Too much to really even comprehend! But what's so cool is that those 4 million minutes are all **ours**—we decide what to do with them! So why not make them awesome and memorable?!

Life is full of decisions. We're constantly having to decide when it comes to sooo many things. "Should I wear this shirt with those jeans, or these shorts with that top? For lunch, should I get spaghetti and meatballs, or the seafood surprise? (I'd go with the spaghetti on that one, guys!) Should I sit here and do my homework, or go outside and shoot some hoops? Should I go talk to that kid who's sitting all alone, or should I just sit with my friends as usual? Should I try out for the swim team? Should I tell him I like him? Should I join this club? Should I be his friend?" From big decisions, to small decisions, to all the ones in between…we have choices to make and it can all get pretty confusing at times. But there is one decision that is MAJOR—one that affects us more than anything—and that is deciding how we are going to live those 4 million minutes, and set the course for the rest of our lives!

So what do I mean by this? Well, I don't mean that we have to sit down and decide on everything we want for our future, but we do need to think about how we want to move through our lives. Will we be positive and try to make the most out of every day, and make growing up fun? (Sounds good, right?) Or will we be negative, and act like "Debbie downers" or "party poopers"? (I'd hope not ☺) I think we can all agree that being positive is the way to go.

What exactly does it mean to *Live High on Life*™?

Living high on *life* is all about being positive—and happy. Sounds pretty simple, right? Happiness is something that everyone strives for in life, but sometimes it seems hard to find. That's why being able to *Live High on Life*™ is so awesome! Because you're capable of creating *your own* happiness, no matter what tough stuff you may be going through. It's all about being happy with yourself and happy with the life you're living. It's about appreciating what you've been given and understanding that each new day is something to look forward to; something to make the most of.

Living high on life means that you're able to keep a healthy and happy mind, body, and spirit by taking care of yourself in several different ways. Mentally, you know that your attitude is everything and that you can make your life what you want it to be. Physically, you realize that it's so important to take care of your body and give it the respect and attention it needs and deserves. And spiritually, you see that you have a purpose in life and that you are most definitely here for a reason. It's about understanding that YOU are in control, and you decide your attitude each day, the choices you make, the goals you want to set for yourself, and the person you want to be. These 12 chapters help explain **how** to *Live High on Life*™ and create for yourself the one thing that everyone is looking for—happiness. ☺

"Every great dream begins with a dreamer. Always remember, you have within you the strength, the patience, and the passion to reach for the stars and change the world."

–Harriet Tubman

Introduction

Have you ever thought about how often we use writing as a way to communicate? In a way, we are all authors. Just like you, I'm the author of a lot things, including many book reports for Mrs. Rookey's English class, notes to friends that I secretly pass during class, awesome wall posts and status updates on Facebook, and never-ending text messages—but what I'm most proud of writing is this book.

Now I'm not sure how you ended up with this book; maybe it was a gift from an adult who cares about you, or maybe the cover caught your eye so you decided to buy it yourself; maybe you saw it on my website or on Facebook, or better yet, maybe you saw me on Oprah! (Haha I wish! Maybe someday!) The point is, however this book ended up in your hands, I'm excited that it did. I mean, that's the whole point of writing a book, right? ... For people to read it. Anyway, maybe you love to read, or maybe you're a lot like me, and you only read books from time to time, or

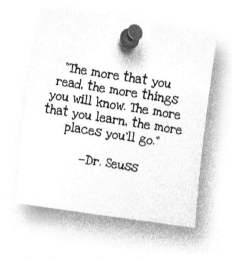

"The more that you read, the more things you will know. The more that you learn, the more places you'll go."

–Dr. Seuss

if it's required reading for school. Although I don't read as often as some people, I've learned from writing this book, that reading is an incredible thing, and can open your eyes to so much! So whether you're a frequent reader, an occasional reader, or not much of a reader at all, I honestly hope that you will *at least* read bits and pieces, because this book is different. It has tips and quotes, and inspiring stories from other teens. So there's a lot of stuff in here that I think can be really helpful and fun for *any* teen to read.

So who am I? And why should you read what I wrote anyway? And why did I decide to spend practically my entire junior and senior years of high school writing this book? Well, my name is Becca (surprise, surprise), and I'm a teenager, just like you. It all started one day during my junior year of high school. I was 16 years old. My aunt Pam was visiting from out of town, and I was reading to her something from my journal. It was an entry I had written about what I thought were the "secrets" to getting through the tough, yet exciting years of growing up. I had written about different situations that my friends and I had been through, and about what I thought were the best ways to deal with these, and how to make the most out of our teenage years. Her face lit up, and she seemed so impressed. She even told me that what I had written could be added on to, and made into a book. But of course I figured that she was just saying that because I'm her niece. As I kept reading, she wouldn't stop describing how amazed she was, and that was all she talked about the rest of her visit here. "Oh Becky, what you wrote is great. You should really consider writing an inspiring book for teens," she said.

At first, I thought she was crazy. I mean really, who would want to hear what *I* had to say? I'm not some famous author, and I barely pass any of my grammar tests in English. How the heck would I ever write a book!? I'm just a regular teen. But it was that very statement that led me to write this book. I am, in every way, just a regular teen, who loves to write, and loves to help people. (I also love sleeping in late, texting, going to Friday night football games at school, hanging out with my friends, and the list goes on and on...) But I figured that maybe it was time to share what has helped me get through middle and high school, and how I have been living the "best years of my life" to the fullest.

"Life isn't about finding yourself, it's about creating yourself"

—Anonymous

Thanks to my aunt, I began writing this book, thinking that even if it only changes the life of one person, then I will have achieved my goal. (Now, considering the time and effort I've put into this book, I sure hope it impacts a lot more than one person! Haha, and I hope that you'll be one of them.) As you live these years, take some time to see what this book has to offer. I'm not an adult talking about growing up as I remember it way back when or anything like that. Instead, I'm living this part of life right now, along with you. In fact, my day today has consisted of getting up early, ugh!, going to school, going to work at the YMCA, and then coming home to do homework (not so much fun), and of course checking up on the latest social news on Facebook. Oh yeah, and somewhere along the way, I bought a $5 footlong from Subway (my favorite) and it was delicious! Sounds pretty normal, right? Well anyway, I encourage you to keep reading, and I think you'll find this book entertaining, interesting, and helpful.

Growing up is a time for change, a time for learning, a time for building your future, and of course a time for FUN! Although it seems hard at times, it doesn't have to be. I'm not sixty years old, and I definitely don't have all the wisdom in the world LOL, but I do know this—if you just make the most out of growing up, and focus on staying true to yourself, growing up won't be so bad—in fact, it'll be totally worth it. It worked for me, and several other teens, and if you open up your mind, the *Live High on Life*™ style can do the same thing for you. Hey, if you've read this far, you're already one step closer to living the life that *you* want to live. Life isn't about just waking up one morning, and saying "Hey I found myself; I figured out who I want to be!" We all know it just doesn't happen like that. Instead, at our age, it's a time for learning and growing and ***creating*** ourselves to be the very best people we can be. It's about being happy with who we are and allowing ourselves to *Live High on Life*™. So keep reading, and we'll take this journey together, and I promise this won't be "just a boring book."

Chapter 1. Loving Yourself First

"In order to be happy in all aspects of your life, you first have to be happy with yourself. You can't get the most out of life if you're unhappy with one of its biggest components; yourself."

—Katie, Age 17

I love flying. I always have, and I probably always will. It's so cool looking down and seeing the rolling hills, the winding rivers, and realizing that there are actually people down there, going on with their daily lives. Meanwhile you're sitting in an airplane, able to take a glimpse at hundreds of towns in minutes, and several states in just hours. It can be pretty neat if you ask me. In a sense, you feel larger than life. It's a great reminder that the world is endless, and that there's so much more to life than we think. I know a lot of people who are afraid to fly, and I can see where they're coming from. It's fun to go from zero to 150 miles per hour at takeoff, as long as it's a smooth takeoff, but when it's bumpy and turbulent, it's not always a calming experience. Then there's always that little fear of "what if something goes wrong?"

This morning I caught a 5 AM flight from North Carolina to Connecticut. It was definitely a little early for me, but I was so excited about visiting family and friends up there. When I got settled on the plane, I looked around and made some quick observations of the people around me; my fellow fly-ees. It was a fairly small plane, and each row sat just two people. I wasn't anxious about flying, but I was anxious to see who was going to sit next to me, since I was flying by myself. A man walked up to my row and gave me a funny look. "Oops," I thought to myself. I figured that maybe I had sat in the wrong seat. "Are you 7F?" he asked me in a confused tone. "Yeah, I think so," I replied hopefully. He hesitantly squeezed his carry-on bag into the slot above

"Make the most of yourself, for that is all there is of you."

—Ralph Waldo Emerson

our heads, and sat down quietly with a book and a bag of peanut M&M's. For a grown man, he seemed awfully worried about flying. I wondered if maybe it was his first time flying. He asked me if I took that flight often, and if I'd ever been on a plane that small. He seemed really worried, and a little surprised about the size of the plane. I told him I'd flown on a plane this size, and that everything went smoothly, but his uncertainty didn't seem to go away.

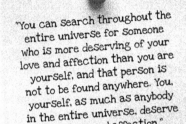

I continued to read my *Seventeen* magazine, while the man next to me anxiously peered all around the plane, probably still worried about the flight. The flight attendant stood up and demonstrated how to buckle the seatbelt, showed where the emergency exits were, and then pulled out the "sample version" of the taxi-yellow airplane oxygen mask. The man next to me looked at me as if a swarm of bees had just flown into his mouth and down his throat. I wondered how I'd make it for hours

"You can search throughout the entire universe for someone who is more deserving of your love and affection than you are yourself, and that person is not to be found anywhere. You, yourself, as much as anybody in the entire universe, deserve your love and affection."

–Buddha

sitting next to someone so afraid of something that I felt so nonchalant about. But that was it, it wasn't a big deal to me; to me it was super exciting. But to him, maybe it was the scariest thing he'd ever done, and I gained a little sympathy for the man. I heard the flight attendant casually announce "… before helping others, you must first make sure that *your* oxygen mask is secured tightly." I thought, "hmm that seems a little selfish. Wouldn't you want to help the people around you, and make sure they're okay too?" But then I realized, if something were to happen, and the man next to me was panicking, I'd need to be able to help myself before I'd be able to help him.

It made perfect sense. That's when I realized that the concept applied to other situations in life too. I know, I know, that might sound like a pretty far-fetched analogy haha. I mean I go from talking about funny-looking oxygen masks on airplanes to talking about loving yourself. But when you think about it, it makes sense. Obviously on a plane, the reason you have to put on your *own* oxygen mask *first*, is because if you're not taking care of yourself, then you wouldn't be able to help others. It's the same in life. If you want to accomplish anything in life, you have to be happy and confident with yourself. You have to love yourself, and take care of yourself. In order to focus on getting good grades, or winning that soccer game, or helping one of your best friends deal with a tough time, you first need to take full responsibility for the one thing in life that *you* control— and that's *you*. Before dealing with the rest of your life, you need to be stable with yourself.

If something had happened to the plane, and I had to help that man sitting next to me, I'd have to take care of myself first.

Loving ourselves may seem like a pretty simple concept, and it definitely comes easily to some people. But to others, it can be fairly difficult. At our age, we can get down on ourselves so easily because the opinions of others really affect us. Sometimes, it can be really hard to feel like you're good enough. It can also be hard to find that essential balance. If you love yourself tooooo much, then you end up being cocky, conceited, or arrogant. But if you don't love yourself *enough*, then you can end up with really low self-confidence and low self-esteem. So balance is extremely important!

So how exactly can we do that? How can we love ourselves? Well, I could write several deep and philosophical paragraphs rambling on about how to gain self-worth and why it is so important. But for most teens, that would be pretty boring. So instead, I decided to make a list of 20 things that you can start doing today! In fact, you can start right this minute! I promise that if you do all the things on this list, you *will* love yourself more than you ever thought possible. I even made a little check list to help keep track. Check it out…

☐ **1. Make a list of 27 things you like about yourself.**

Why 27? Well, because it's my lucky number haha. And if you come up with 27, you're off to a great start! In your list, try to think of physical and, well, non-physical things. You don't actually have to write them down if you don't want to. You could just keep a mental list. But if you do write them down, it'll help you see the positives about yourself! And you can even keep adding onto your list as you think of things. Try to get to 100! Think that's crazy? Well it's not! You'd be surprised…you *can* do it. Just try.

☐ **2. Focus on the positives, not the negatives. Always.**

Too often we spend so much time thinking about the things we *don't* like about ourselves, that we forget about the millions of *great* things about ourselves. Next time you're tempted to make a negative comment to yourself, shut it out, and immediately think about one of the things on your list of positives! Sure, it's easy to be hard on ourselves and find the things we wish we could change. But if we constantly kept *wishing* to change something here, or something else there, then we wouldn't even be ourselves anymore. So think about the good things. Always. Don't let yourself be negative.

☐ **3. Don't let other people break the relationship you have with yourself.**

The relationship you have with yourself is more important that *any* relationship you will ever have! Don't ever let anyone else ruin it. You're the one who ultimately decides how you'll feel about yourself. So if someone tries to bring you down in any way, shape, or form, remember that you're the one in control and they can't come between you and yourself. Ignore negative comments. Block out stupid remarks. Make sure that this relationship is your top priority, because you can't fully commit to other relationships until you first have a strong relationship with yourself.

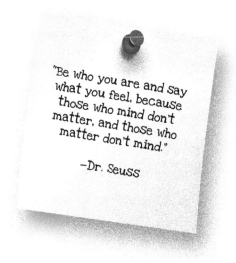

"Be who you are and say what you feel, because those who mind don't matter, and those who matter don't mind."

–Dr. Seuss

☐ **4. Compliment yourself every single day.**

When you wake up in the morning, before you even get, jump, hop, or roll out of bed, think of at least one confidence-booster! Doing this can help set the stage for a good day! And throughout the day, think of some more.

☐ **5. Go an entire day without thinking anything negative about yourself.**

Try it. For some of us, it may be a piece of cake, but for others, it may seem nearly impossible. Whether you know you *can*, or think you *can't*, do it anyway. And if any little negative comments try to slip their way in, knock them out of the way with something positive. When you get through an entire day, do the same thing the next day, and the next day, and the next day, and in less than a month, all that positive thinking will become a habit. Really! It's like magic, haha. But don't just make it a habit; also make it a **promise to yourself** that you will go without putting yourself down in any way.

p.s.- start #5 today for sure!

☐ **6. Put little reminders in your life...**

...to let yourself know that you *are* worth something, and that you *are* an awesome person! Leave a note on your mirror, your bed post, your laptop, your bedroom door, or any other place you look at often. Write something that you're happy with about yourself, like "I am a great friend to others," or "I am happy with my body" (I got this idea from my first college roommate who was overcoming an eating disorder! Leaving little sticky-note reminders worked for her, and I thought it was a great idea for reminding us of the things we love about ourselves! Thanks for the idea, Dev!) Or leave little reminders in other places...like your car dashboard, or your school notebooks and binders!

"Love yourself first and everything else falls into line. You really have to love yourself to get anything done in this world."

–Lucille Ball

☐ **7. Decorate *your* space *your* way.**

Make a collage or poster (or even just decorate a piece of paper) with quotes, pictures, magazines clippings, drawings, or words that describe you and what you love about yourself or what makes you unique! For this project, don't even think about how you think *others* view you. Think about positive ways *you* feel about yourself. This poster/collage/whatever-you-want-it-to-be should be all about you. Define and describe yourself, and hang it somewhere where you can see it each day. But remember, try not to focus on the negatives. Think positively.

☐ **8. Don't be afraid of change—it's part of learning and growing.**

Sometimes, itty bitty changes in our lives can make us feel refreshed and energized. Switch things up sometimes to give yourself a fresh start. Re-arrange your room, use a different shampoo or soap, listen to a different genre of music or a new artist, try eating different foods, meet new people, make a new friend, go on a date with somebody who is really different from you (just make sure it's a safe decision—don't choose anyone too crazy haha), find a new form of exercise to add on to your usual routine, wear an outfit that you normally wouldn't consider, or change your hairstyle. Obviously these are just a few of many, many things you could do to change stuff up a bit. The point here is that being a teen is all about experiencing different things and learning about what we like and don't like and what's good for us, and what's not. So by experiencing things *different* from our norm, we learn *more* about ourselves!

☐ **9. Do what *you* love.**

This one is pretty much self-explanatory. Because it doesn't say "Do what mom and dad love," or "Do what your boyfriend or girlfriend loves," or "Do what all the celebrities love." It says "Do what *you* love" because you're the one who gets to decide—so you might as well do things that you actually want to do. If you love to run cross country and want to go out for the team, but your best friend thinks you should play soccer, choose cross country. If your date orders sushi and you hate sushi, don't order sushi just to "fit in." Order the food *you* want—even if it's kid's chicken nuggets and fries. I'm guilty of that one, haha. If you want to be a teacher, but your parents want you to be a doctor, choose to be a teacher. Choose to do what you love. If the clothes that are in style don't appeal to you, don't go along with it just because that's "what's in right now." Make your own style. Do what you want. That leads right into #10…

☐ **10. Be a trend setter.**

Usually when we think of a trend setter, we think of someone who sets fashion trends that others follow. And although that's true, that's not all I mean by "Be a trend setter." What I mean by this is, do your own thing and do what makes you happy—even if it's not what everyone else is doing. So yes, when it comes to clothes or hairstyles, you should be

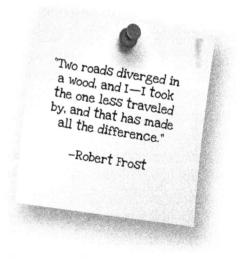

"Two roads diverged in a wood, and I—I took the one less traveled by, and that has made all the difference."

–Robert Frost

a trend setter. You should dress and look the way that makes you feel the most comfortable and happy with yourself. For some of us, following the latest trends is what we like to do. For others, it isn't. Either way, it's our decision. It's just important to do what we want.

But we can trend set in other ways too—like with our attitude and actions. Trend setting in this way is all about being a leader and a role model for our peers and the people around us. When we trend set attitude and action, we do and say what *we* feel and know is right. Want an example? Here you go...

Everyone is sitting at the lunch table talking and laughing about the party Nick had last weekend. A new girl at school, Sarah, walks up to the table and is about to sit down. Nick and his friends snicker and one girl, Allison, whispers, "Who does this new girl think she is? She can't just come sit with us—we don't even know her and she doesn't look so cool..." The kids at the table laugh. Sarah hears Allison and then quickly draws a blank. She turns around and begins to walk away when Jessie yells out, "Wait, you don't have to go. Don't listen to Allison, she's just in one of her moods. You can come sit with us. What's your name?" Sarah walks back over and after two kids scoot over to make room for her, Sarah sits down at the lunch table. Suddenly, everyone wants to know more about the new girl that Jessie invited to the table.

☐ **11. Do good things for others.**

Out of all the ways to love yourself, this is actually one of my favorites. It's probably the fastest and easiest way to feel better about yourself! And the reason for that is simple—when you help others out, or make other people feel good, it makes you feel twice as good. There's nothing better than knowing that you made someone else happy. So #11 is awesome because it's win-win. You *and* the person you make happy benefit from this! So what can you do? Well, when it comes to doing good things for others, I don't even know where to begin. There are SO many things you can do. Compliment the people around you, lend a listening ear to a friend, figure out what volunteer or service projects you could get involved in, respect those different from you... Simply be kind towards others, and by doing that, you're actually being kind to yourself, too!

☐ **12. Surround yourself with people who lift you up...**

...not with people who bring you down. The ones you spend the most time around are the ones who affect your own attitude and actions. So make sure that you hang out with people who support you, care about you, and want the best for you. Those are true friends. People who try to make you do stuff you don't want to do, or people who put you down are the ones to steer clear of. Their negativity can affect who *you* are. Find people who love and accept you for *you,* and always, always, always remember that you should never feel like you have to change who you are for anyone else.

☐ **13. Quote yourself**

Most famous quotes are from (surprise, surprise) famous people. But they don't have to be. I love quotes and always have because they're like snapshots of inspiration through words. Quotes can mean a lot, and many famous people are remembered by just a few quotes. And those quotes tell a whole lot about what type of people they are. So pretend for a sec. that you had to come up with **one single quote** to be remembered by. What would it be? Think about it for a little while and then write it in the sticky-note above. After all, you are rare—there is only one *you,* so you are *just as important* as any famous person who has ever been quoted! Here's mine…

write your OWN quote here:

"Don't change yourself just for the rest of the world. Change the rest of the world just by being yourself."

☐ **14. Be honest with yourself.**

Most of us wouldn't lie to our friends and family, so why lie to ourselves? It's just as bad—if not worse. Being able to be honest with yourself is a must if you want to have a good relationship with yourself. This means, if you know deep down that you shouldn't do something—don't lie to yourself; be honest with yourself. Follow your instinct. Sometimes it's hard for us to do that, because sometimes we don't like admitting the truth to ourselves. If the truth isn't what we want, then we try to block it out of our heads. But by doing that, it only makes things worse. Example time…

Let's say Jillian is dating a guy who she knows isn't right for her. They argue a lot, he treats her like dirt, and he brings down her spirits. But since Jillian has been with him for so long, she's scared to leave him. She knows that he's not right for her, and she knows that she should break up with him—but she continually lies to herself because she doesn't want to face the truth that's inside of her.

By Jillian staying with her boyfriend, she's not being honest with herself, and that can lead to even more serious problems down the road. Go with your instincts; go with your gut. And don't ever be afraid to admit the truth to yourself. Just like in every other relationship, honesty is everything!

☐ **15. Take time for yourself**

This is actually what Chapter 5 is all about, but it definitely belongs on this checklist too! Taking time for yourself is one of the greatest things you can do. Everyone needs down time, alone time, and quiet time, and it's so important to remember to set time aside for that. There are many ways to do this… you can exercise, dance, write, do art, meditate, do yoga, go on nature walks (my favorite—nature is one of the best ways to clear your head!), or take a nap; pretty much anything that you find relaxing and calming is great. Take a break from Facebook, MySpace, Twitter, cell phones, and any other technology that may consume too much of your time. This is the time to reflect on your day, and focus on yourself. Put your stress, worries, and responsibilities to the back of your mind and just chill! Whatever type of "you-time" you prefer is fine; just make sure you actually make time for it.

"What lies behind us and what lies before us are tiny matters compared to what lies within us."

–Ralph Waldo Emerson

☐ **16. Love your body; it's a huge part of who you are**

I'll talk a lot more about this later on in Chapter 9, but just like #15, #16 needs to be included in this list too! Our bodies definitely have a **whole lot** to do with the way we view ourselves. A lot of times when we have low self-esteem, it's body-related. But when we have the strength to love our bodies for what they are, we reach a *major* accomplishment! Just as I mentioned earlier, focus on the positives; NOT the negatives! More importantly, make sure that you're taking care of your body by exercising, making healthy decisions, eating right, and getting enough sleep (and you and I both know that sleepin' isn't hard for us teens to do—just make sure you get enough!) You only get one body, so treat it right!

☐ **17. Don't compare yourself to others.**

"When you are content to be simply yourself and don't compare or compete, everybody will respect you."

—Lao-Tzu

The other day I was babysitting an adorable 5-year-old (well, she would have you know that she's actually 5 ½). Anyway, we were watching TV and a commercial for some type of shampoo was on. In the commercial, there was a woman with long, wavy, blonde hair doing the hair-flip thing. That's when the 5-year-old cutie pie looked at me and said "Becca, whose hair is prettier? Hers or mine? Hers is, right? Because she's a model." I couldn't believe that a *5-year-old* was actually comparing herself to some model on TV! I feel like that's a little early to be worrying about whose hair is prettier. The thing is, it's natural to compare ourselves to others. But we have to be careful, because we can end up feeling badly about ourselves if we compare too often, especially if we compare in a negative way. So try not to compare yourself to other people, because you are unique, and there is no comparison to any of us.

☐ **18. Accept compliments.**

When people compliment you on something, actually take it to heart. Don't just shrug it off and tell yourself "oh that's not true," or "oh they don't really mean that." Most likely, they totally mean it, or they wouldn't have said it. So believe it and accept it and use compliments from others as a way to truly feel better about yourself.

☐ **19. Don't ever settle for less than what you deserve.**

Too often teens let their low self-confidence get in the way of knowing what they deserve. Don't be one of those people. Know that you are great and that you deserve the best. Don't settle for people picking on you, don't settle for an abusive relationship, don't settle for bad decisions, and don't settle for low self-esteem. Remember who you are and what you deserve. Keep the bar raised high, and don't settle for less than what you know you really deserve!

☐ **20. Don't just think it... Believe it!**

So a few times in this check list, we came up with things that we love about ourselves. And that's awesome! But they don't mean as much unless we actually believe that they are true. When you tell yourself that you're pretty or handsome, don't just stand there looking in the

"Success is liking yourself, liking what you do, and liking how you do it."

–Maya Angelou

mirror thinking that...actually believe it. When you tell yourself that you're good at something, don't just kinda-sorta think it, but believe it and let others see that you believe it. **Believe in yourself and love yourself** and you will be *amazed* by how much easier and exciting life will be!

At the end of each chapter is a "Write About It" section, where you can do the writing activity, or jot down notes or ideas as you read!

Write About It: Loving Yourself First

Describe yourself in 60 seconds. Make a list of things
that you believe define who you are. Try to get as many as
you can before the time runs out. Start out each one with
"I am..." When you're done, read over what you wrote. It's so
interesting to see how we think of ourselves!

Chapter 2. It's All About Attitude

"Having a positive attitude not only affects the outcome of your endeavors, but it also affects the successs of others. Why waste your time sulking in negativity? Life is so much more fun when you are happy."

—*Hillary, Age 18*

I want to start out this chapter with a short story. It is a Native American legend called *The Wolves Within*, and I think that it shows us why choosing to have a good attitude is so important.

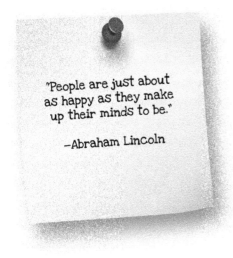

"People are just about as happy as they make up their minds to be."

–Abraham Lincoln

An old Grandfather said to his grandson, who came to him with anger at a friend who had done him an injustice... "Let me tell you a story. I too, at times, have felt great hate for those who have taken so much, with no sorrow for what they do. But hate wears you down, and does not hurt your enemy. It's like taking poison and wishing your enemy would die. I have struggled with these feelings many times. It is as if there are two wolves inside me; one is good and does no harm. He lives in harmony with all around him and does not take offense when no offense was intended. He will only fight when it is right to do so, and in the right way. But the other wolf... ah! The littlest thing will send him into a fit of temper. He fights everyone, all of the time, for no reason. He cannot think because his anger and hate are so great. It is helpless anger, for his anger will change nothing. Sometimes it is hard to live with these two wolves inside me, for both of them try to dominate my spirit." The boy looked intently into his Grandfather's eyes and asked, "Which one wins, Grandfather?" The Grandfather smiled and quietly said, "The one I feed."

Think about this story and its meaning. Do you think it can relate to your life, and your attitude? The different wolves can represent the choices we have to make when it comes to handling situations. We can either "feed the good wolf" by keeping a positive attitude, or, "feed the bad wolf" by having a negative attitude. If we have a bad attitude all the time, then our life may seem terrible, but if we "allow the good wolf to win" then even the toughest situations in our lives seem much better. Our life is all about choices, and although we can't always control what happens in our life, *we choose* how to handle it. We choose which wolf to feed, and determine which wolf wins.

How many times have you heard someone say "life is what you make it?" Probably a lot, right? I know that I have. I guess sometimes it seems like that can get old, but have you ever actually thought about what that means? It's very true and makes a lot of sense. Life really is what you make it, because no matter what situation is thrown at you, whether it be good or bad, *you're* the one who ultimately determines how you deal with it, and that's where attitude comes into play. When it comes to making your life what you want it to be, attitude is the most important part. It's all about attitude! It's obvious that we can't always control the events that happen in our lives, but what we can control is how we react to them.

I think we can all agree that as teens, there is a lot we feel like we have no control over. Like our teacher just randomly deciding to give us a pop quiz that we end up failing. Or our boyfriend or girlfriend breaking up with us for like, no reason. Or finding out that we didn't get into the college of our dreams. Or our best friend going behind our back and doing something totally deceitful. Or our parents dropping the bomb that they're getting divorced. We both know the list could go on, and on, and on. This is one of the toughest, most confusing, and turbulent times of our

"Wherever you go, no matter what the weather, always bring your own sunshine."

–Anthony J. D'Angelo

lives. There are a lot of things that we have to deal with, that we wish we didn't have to. I know for me, sometimes I wish I could just crawl into a hole away from the rest of the world. Or run away, to go live in Disney World, or some island paradise. Haha, what an easy life that would be!

But the truth is, we can't just run away from the hard stuff in our lives. Instead, we have to face reality. The thing about facing reality is that it can go in two different directions, and that direction is determined by our perspective. When something unexpected, difficult, or disappointing happens in our life—whether it's not making the cut for the football team, or losing someone you care about to cancer—we have to face it. And our perspective, or the way we view situations, is what affects our entire life. We can face reality in a negative way, with a bad attitude, and end up taking a low road to a dead end. Or we can face reality in a positive way, with a great attitude, and take the high road—making life a lot more enjoyable! It's not about what we go through that counts; it's about how we handle it that counts. Our attitude is *so* much more powerful than we can even imagine. Let's take a closer look at two different perspectives and how attitude can completely make us, or break us…

During her freshman year of high school, 14-year-old Miranda found out that her mother had breast cancer. When her mom told her the news, she was shocked, and had no idea what to think. At first, the reality of it hadn't really hit Miranda. But as time passed, she realized how serious the cancer was. Miranda was scared, and worried, and hope was hard for her to find. Most of all, she was angry—angry that something like this would happen to her mom. She wanted to get her mind off all the pain. A few of her friends told her to start hanging with them, and that they knew how to make her feel

"Our attitude toward life determines life's attitude towards us."

–John N. Mitchell

better. She started drinking, and tried smoking for the first time. She knew it wasn't the right decision, but she did it anyway, because she was mad, and thought by doing those things, it would make her pain and fear go away. Her mom's cancer got even worse, but Miranda didn't know how to handle it. She hung out with that same group of friends more and more often. And soon the occasional drinking and smoking turned into constant partying. But Miranda thought she was happier—it was her way to get her mind off things. Sadly, Miranda's mom passed away, and Miranda had no idea how to handle it. She started skipping school, and because of that, her grades started slipping. She hung out with a group of friends who pressured her into doing things she didn't want to do. Her old friends realized she was changing, and her family saw it too. Miranda started getting into arguments with the people around her, including her family. She had so much hurt and anger inside of her, that she took it out on everyone else. It was like she hated the entire world. She needed someone to talk to, and had plenty of friends who reached out to her, but Miranda just kept everything bottled up, and her anger and attitude just got worse. Her whole world seemed like it was tumbling down. It took Miranda a whole* *year before she realized she had been going down the wrong path. Luckily, she was able to get herself back on track, with the help and support of her true friends and family. But looking back, Miranda regretted the decisions she had made in the past, and wished that she had dealt with her tough time differently.*

14-year-old Kevin also dealt with his mom's struggle and death from breast cancer during his freshman year of high school. When Kevin first found out, he felt the same way as Miranda—scared, worried, confused, and sad. And over time, as his mom's health got worse, Kevin knew that his mom's time was limited. He spent as much time with his mom and with his family as he could, because there was no telling what the next day would bring. Kevin was full of anger and sadness, because he knew his mom didn't deserve to be going through that. Kevin found friends he could talk to about the situation and that helped him a lot. He even started visiting the counselor at school, who helped keep his spirits up. As much as Kevin wanted to escape everything, he knew he couldn't. He knew that he would have to stick it out and hope for the best. When his mom passed away, Kevin was devastated. He didn't know how he would ever get over the loss of his mother. But instead of just grieving and feeling worse, Kevin got the idea to help others who were going through the same situation that he had been through. He knew that if he had gone through it, then maybe he could provide support for others. So Kevin started volunteering at a local elementary school, helping kids who were dealing with the loss of a loved one. He also helped out with Relay for Life, an event sponsored by the American Cancer Society. Kevin was happy knowing that he was channeling his emotions into helping others. He knew that his mother would be proud of him, and for Kevin, that was the best part of all.

"Attitude is a little thing that makes a big difference."

–Winston Churchill

Miranda and Kevin both had to face the same situation, but the way they handled it was *completely* different. Kevin clearly had a much more positive attitude than Miranda. Miranda let her anger build up, and took it out on others. She also made a lot of stupid decisions that she ended up regretting. Kevin was just as sad and upset as Miranda, but instead of making things worse, he was determined to find something positive out of the situation.

Same situation + 2 different attitudes = *Completely* different outcome

Negative situation + Positive attitude = Better outcome

Negative situation + Negative attitude = Negative outcome

We all learn in math that a negative plus a negative is STILL a negative. A negative plus a negative *cannot* equal a positive. But a negative plus a positive *can* equal a positive, and that same rule applies to our lives. Sometimes, things happen that we aren't exactly happy about, but that's part of life, and you can make it SO much better just by having a positive attitude. Of course there are certain emotions that we just can't control, but attitude and emotions are two separate things. When you cry, that reflects emotion, but when you take a tough situation out on others (like Miranda did), that reflects attitude. See the difference?

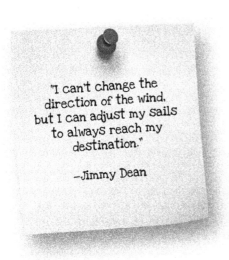

"I can't change the direction of the wind, but I can adjust my sails to always reach my destination."

—Jimmy Dean

When we're going through something tough, it's hard not to let our emotions get the best of us. But when we have a positive attitude about even the worst situations, we may learn and grow as people in ways we never thought imaginable. Let's look at this next story and check out Sarah's advice for teens going through a struggling time.

My dad has always been my best friend. He always understands me, always supports me, and always makes me smile. We were always really close. He was my protector, my rock, and my daddy. But all of that came crashing down on December 26, 2007. He left our family for God knows where. He told my mom he wanted a divorce, and that he wanted something more. I was devastated. The man I had known for so long was all of a sudden someone I didn't recognize. He moved far away to California. We later found out that he had been having an affair. I never expected my dad, who loved my mom so passionately, to be with another woman. With no one to provide for the family, we moved away; away from the pain; away from the place of abandonment. I left my friends, my home, and my heart behind. For months I was plagued with depression, confusion, and wounds that wouldn't heal. We all pulled our resources together to make up for the void my dad had left in the family. I realized that I had to shut off my emotions if I was going to *move on. Well, I thought this would work, and it did for a while. But then I found myself becoming a hollow, robot-like person. Life had left me; my dad had left me. This was the hardest experience of my life. Despite a year of darkness, loneliness, and confusion, my family is whole once again. I am no longer lifeless, but full of life and love. What got me through were my faith and my family. As I reflect on that time in my life, I see the good that has to be born of such pain. If you are going through a time of loss, hopelessness, or abandonment, **remember that you will learn something valuable.** Don't get caught up in yourself, but invest in others. Have faith, and don't give up!*

—Sarah, Age 17

Sarah knew her family would never be exactly the same as it was before. What happened with her dad, happened, and that was just a fact. But by Sarah having a good attitude about it, she realized that there was something good that came from that situation. She learned **a lot** and grew as a person, and her whole family grew from that as well. Although her emotions took over her life for some time, she stepped back and told herself that she couldn't be depressed forever. She knew she had to find the good among the bad, even if it seemed hard to find. She found support from friends and allowed her faith to help her get through her tough time. Sarah's story shows that every cloud has a silver lining if you strive to have a positive attitude. No matter how big or small that silver lining may be, it is there somewhere in every situation...You can find something good in *everything* if you just look hard enough!

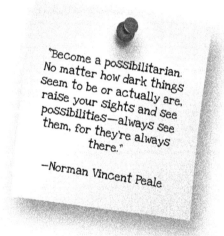

"Become a possibilitarian. No matter how dark things seem to be or actually are, raise your sights and see possibilities—always see them, for they're always there."

—Norman Vincent Peale

18-year-old Olivia has been able to find the "silver lining" in her struggle with a learning difference called dyslexia...

I have always struggled through school and it's not because I don't try; it's because I have a learning difference. In the 3rd grade I was diagnosed with dyslexia, and it changed my life in so many ways. It was a relief that I wasn't dumb; I learn differently than most students. Because of my learning difference I had to work ten times harder than my friends, I had to go to tutoring, and I was always after school with my teachers trying to bring my grades up. I was fortunate enough to have amazing parents who have stood by me and have always been there to help. I am also very grateful to my friends because without them, I don't think I would have made it in a public school. They are always there to help me in class. Even though I have had a great support system, that doesn't help with the struggles I've had to face every day. It's hard being in the advanced classes with my friends who always get A's without even studying, while I would study for hours and get C's and D's. And even though my parents are great, my dyslexia caused us to fight all the time because I really just wanted to be normal and not have this daily fight with myself. Now after 10 years of having dyslexia **I have realized that my learning difference is really a gift, which I'm very thankful for!** Being normal is boring and even though I've had to work harder and study harder than everyone else, I'm glad I had to! Because now as I'm about to head off to college, **I realize that those skills, and my work ethics that I've gained from being dyslexic, will pay off.** The one thing I can tell you is you should never feel bad for someone who has a learning disability because it is a gift! When you have a learning disability you are able to think of things in a different way. Yes in school, it sucks sometimes, but in life, it's amazing! Overcoming dyslexia is a daily struggle and I'm still fighting to conquer it, but the best way to overcome something is to have a great support system and to not be afraid to talk to someone about it, because it really does help. Now I am proud to say I am dyslexic and that I have almost overcome it and **it's not a dark thing in my life; it's the bright light that makes me different!**

"Things turn out best for the people who make the best out of the way things turn out."

–Art Linkletter

—Olivia, Age 18

Even though Olivia has had a constant struggle with dyslexia for a long time, she found something good out of it. She realized that her work habits of studying often and having to work extra-hard will pay off for her in the future. She may have to work harder than her peers to get good grades, but she never felt sorry for herself or let her learning disability hold her back. She has kept a great attitude about it, and that's what is ultimately allowing her to overcome it!

The next story, from 16-year-old Kyle, sums up exactly why having a positive attitude can completely turn your life around…

I was in foster care for a total of two years; this was the roughest time I have experienced thus far in my life. Although it was filled with troubles, concerns, and worries, I figured out a way to keep a good attitude throughout these two very long years. I found a constructive way to cope with foster care—music. Music was my outlet whenever I had too much on my mind. All I would have to do was put a Beatles album into my Sony portable C.D. player and lie back and listen. It would take me away from all my troubles and cleared my head temporarily. This helped stabilize my thoughts and motivated me to sustain hope in my situation. In my opinion when going through tough times, keeping a good outlook or attitude is mandatory and music helped my attitude greatly.

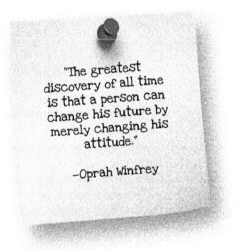

"The greatest discovery of all time is that a person can change his future by merely changing his attitude."

–Oprah Winfrey

Self-pity is NOT an option either. I stayed with many different kids in my situation in group homes and foster homes who used their poor childhood as an excuse to do poorly in school and just make bad decisions in general. In my experience, that was never an option; I always tried my hardest and when I pulled through, the feeling of success was overwhelming. It feels good for me to look back and remember the bad conditions of the foster care situation and know that I made it through them, while sustaining a positive attitude towards life. You have to stay strong, and you also have to learn to be independent in your thoughts. When I was in foster care dozens of people were always trying to tell me how to feel and how to be happy. I learned to take everything I was told and put it in my pocket with a grain of salt. I saw psychologists, social workers, home guardians, and foster parents—all with a different message—and at the age of twelve it was quite overwhelming and scary. I kept my goals in mind and pursued them no matter what the situation.

I also had someone I could always lean on when I was in foster care and could always talk to—my brother Eric. I could vent to him and he could vent to me and we would help each other. I would recommend finding someone you can talk to because it feels good to get thoughts or feelings off your mind when in such messed up situations. It feels good to know someone is there for you and has your back; a feeling of security, if you will. These are just a few strategies that I used when I was going through a tough childhood experience. My advice to other teens or children that are in a poor situation is first to find a positive mental escape method. Music was and will always be mine, but it could be writing, reading, exercise, or anything constructive that can keep your mind off the troublesome situation for a while. Also take stories like mine and use them as tools to pull through, keep up hope, and maintain a good attitude. All will be o.k. Just stay strong and you will make it through. This is advice that I still use to this day.

—*Kyle, The Travers Brothers Band lead guitarist, Age 16*

Kyle didn't *choose* to be placed in foster care, but that was something beyond his control. Although he was faced with such a rough experience, he found a healthy outlet to help him deal with his emotions, and that was music. He kept a positive attitude all throughout, and that has made a *world* of difference. Like Kyle said, there are several other ways to keep a good attitude, including trying to get your mind off the situation by doing something else like writing, or reading, or exercising. What are some of the activities *you* do that make you feel good? For Kyle, and his brother Eric, music is what got them through. But there are several other ways to keep a positive attitude while going through a tough time. Here are 3 simple and healthy ways to keep your spirits up:

1. **Clear Your Head—**

    Try to veer away from dwelling in the situation. Find something to do to get your mind off it. *You* control your attitude, and if you step away from the situation and find other things to do, it will make you feel better. Art, music, exercise, dance, writing, reading, being outside in nature, meditation, journaling…these are all examples of things you can do to handle your emotions. Can you think of some others? I know a lot of my friends who were going through stuff at home would try to find things in the community to get involved in so they weren't just sitting at home all day. Like doing the school musical, getting a job, playing sports, or joining a volunteer club or service group. If you still have trouble controlling your attitude or getting your mind off something, **then talk to someone**. A friend, a teacher, a parent, a counselor…someone who cares and will listen. It feels SO good to get stuff off your chest. And that way, instead of bottling up emotions that cause you to have a crappy attitude, you let it all out, allowing you to start fresh with a positive perspective.

2. Think Towards the Future—

I used to hear this saying—"All will be okay in the end. If it's not okay, then it's not the end." At first, I never really believed that, but as I got older, I started to see that it is true. No matter what difficult things we encounter, whether they're big or small, they will get better in time. Time is the one thing that makes things seem harder...because we can't just hit a button and be 10 years down the road into our future. Instead, we have to live those years and make it through any obstacles we come across in the meantime. We have to be patient, and let time run its course. But everything truly will get better in time. If you're going through something tough, or if you

"Keep your face to the sunshine and you cannot see the shadow."

—Helen Adams Keller

ever have, you probably know how hard it can be to keep a good attitude. But every single day when you wake up, just remember that it is a brand NEW day, and you can make it out to be what you want, based on your perspective and attitude. Think about how years from now, some of the things we go through at our age *won't even matter!* Like who was prom queen, or who dated whom, or who got the lead in the play. These things seem like a big deal when we're young, but that all changes when everyone graduates and moves on. So don't sweat the small stuff, stay positive about the tough stuff, and remember that there is so much more to life than we can even imagine. We have bright futures ahead of us, and they will be awesome!

3. Try to Find the Silver Lining—

Yeah, I know, that's totally not easy. And it probably seems *impossible* to find a positive side to some situations. But no matter what the situation is, there is always one guaranteed silver lining!!! And that is, that you always *learn* from every single experience you ever go through. Learning and growing as a person—that's a very positive thing. So even if you think nothing good can come from a certain situation, just remember that **if nothing else, you'll learn from it**. Something, anything—maybe learn a lot, or maybe learn a little, or maybe you won't even realize you learned something until years down the road—but either way, learning is an essential ingredient to growing and becoming a better person. So try to find something positive in every situation; try to find that silver lining; but if you feel like you *really* can't, then just know that you've learned and grown from the situation, and that is a truly great thing to accomplish in itself!

We are lucky to be able to control our attitudes, so it's important to take advantage of that, and use the power of our attitudes to help us be the best people we can be. If we want to *get* the most out of our teenage years, then we have to *make* the most of our teenage years. And our attitude is what will determine that. So choose wisely. ☺

Write About It: It's All About Attitude

Think of a time when you had a bad attitude about something. Why did you react the way you did? What could you have done differently? What will you do in the future to make sure that you keep a positive attitude during tough situations?

Chapter 3. You're Here for a Reason

A few years ago I had to do a scrapbook project for my freshmen English class—a scrapbook of my entire life. I remember when my teacher assigned the project and how excited I was to be able to turn my life into a piece of art. Filled with pictures, quotes, colorful stickers and paper cutouts, it was the perfect opportunity to look back on all of my experiences and put my memories together into a scrapbook about my life! And I mean, who doesn't love going through old photos?! On top of including stuff from our past, our teacher had us write something new for each year, whether it was a poem, a reflection, or a personal story. One of the final writing assignments for our scrapbook was to write a letter to ourselves. We had to write about what we thought was our purpose in life. I was 14 years old when I wrote that letter. How was I supposed to have any idea what my purpose in life even was!?

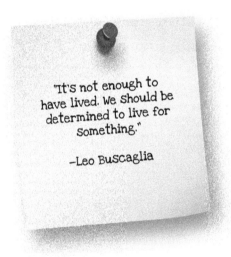

"It's not enough to have lived. We should be determined to live for something."

—Leo Buscaglia

Being 14 was tough, to say the least. Being a freshman wasn't easy, and certainly wasn't always fun. There were mean girls, hard teachers, intimidating upperclassmen, and immature boys who thought it was fun to break hearts. I remember that year being one of the most difficult times of growing up and I can promise you that thinking about my "life purpose" was probably the last thing on my mind. But I knew I had to come up with something for my English class, and so I did. I clearly remember trying to write that letter; *trying* is the key word here… because I sat there for hours and had no idea what to say. At 14, I could tell you how to make EasyMac, and how to change my MySpace layout, but when it came to more complex stuff, like telling you my purpose in life, I didn't really have an answer.

Sure, I thought about my future and what I wanted to do with my life, but I had a million different ideas. I wanted to be a teacher, work for the Travel Channel going all over the world to taste different types of food, be a singer, a writer, a news anchor, a chef, a dancer, an actor, an environmentalist, have my own daytime talk show, and the list seemed to go on and on and on. But when it came to really thinking about my reason for being here, it wasn't so easy to come up with ideas. I thought if I became a doctor or scientist,

I could find a cure for cancer, and that would be a pretty cool purpose, right? But I also thought that it just wasn't the job for me. Even though the world could definitely use more scientists, doctors and nurses, it wasn't something I wanted to do. It wasn't my purpose. I started to think of what I'm good at, and what I love. And that's where I found my answer.

> "Don't ask what the world needs. Ask what makes you come alive, and go do it. Because what the world needs is people who have come alive."
>
> —Howard Thurman

Sometimes it's hard for us to believe and it's not always easy to recognize, but we're all incredibly unique and we **all** have reasons for being here. You weren't an accident and neither was I, and understanding that is so important. There are so many times when we feel worthless and self-conscious, but remembering that we play a huge role in our lifetime helps keep our eyes focused and our heads held high. So if someone were to ask you right now what your purpose in life is, what would you say? Would you have an immediate answer, or would it take you a little longer to respond. Or would you even have an answer at all? If you already know what you want to do with your life, that's awesome! You should definitely embrace that and live for what you love doing. But if you're still unsure like most of us, that's cool too! I knew I didn't have a definite answer to write about in my letter, but I did come to the conclusion that I wanted to do what I love, because I thought that would be the best contribution I could give to this world.

> "You have brains in your head. You have feet in your shoes. You can steer yourself in any direction you choose. You're on your own. And you know what you know. You are the guy who'll decide where to go."
>
> —Dr. Seuss

Even though parents, teachers, and friends seem to be constantly reminding us of the pressures and responsibilities that lead to "success," it's important to make sure that you're not just doing what they want you to do or doing something just because you think it's expected of you. Work, college, and what we want to do with our future are conversations that come up all the time. We have so much pressure placed on us and sometimes it makes us feel like we're not completely in control of our lives.

Not to mention, it adds *a lot* of stress! But we are in control, and we just have to remember that. And when it comes to our future and our life, it's our responsibility to truly make it ours. We have the choice to either do what other people want us to do, or to do what we love. Wouldn't you rather do something you love!?

"Follow your passion, and success will follow you."

—Terri Guillemets

Your purpose is what you make it. Just like Howard Thurman said, "what the world needs is people who have come alive." Why not become one of those people? Find something you enjoy, or something you have an interest in, and build on that. If you love something enough, you can get better and better at it. It's all about trying and putting in effort. **You** are the one who has to make it happen. So right now, think of some things you're good at, or things you're interested in. How can you get better at them? What steps can you take? We all have to start somewhere, right? By expanding our horizons and by excelling in things we're passionate about, we gain confidence and learn to love ourselves and others more.

You can make a difference in the world just by doing what you love! Find what you're passionate about, and stick with it. If you love a sport, keep playing. Learn new skills and practice more often. Push yourself to be the best. If you love cooking, make up your own recipes and share them with other people. Make yourself stand out. Find ways to be involved with others who share common interests or similar gifts. I love how Oprah put it: "Surround yourself with people who lift you higher." That is soooo true! People who care about you and what you're doing will encourage you and help you get where you want to go.

"Choose a job you love and you will never have to work a day in your life."

—Confucius

Think of careers you could go into that are related to what you love. Don't just settle for what is easiest or the most convenient. Try to go above and beyond and combine that effort with something you enjoy. All of your hard work will be well worth it in the end! And don't ever give up because someone else wants you to, or because you don't believe in yourself. Those definitely aren't good enough excuses. It's easy to feel like we're going to be "stuck" doing something in our future that we don't want to do, but when we have goals and ambition, creating a future full of something we love seems a whole lot more realistic. It's not always about where you come from; it's about where you're going. The past is the past, and even though it has helped shape us into who we are now, it doesn't have to define who we want to be. Define yourself. And if you think there's nothing special about you, you'd better think again!

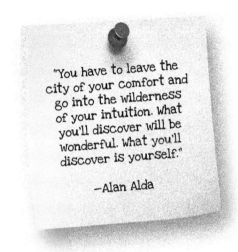

"You have to leave the city of your comfort and go into the wilderness of your intuition. What you'll discover will be wonderful. What you'll discover is yourself."

–Alan Alda

Believe that you're here because you're meant to do something important. Because that's the *truth*! Whether we want to or not, we all contribute to the world in some way or another, so why not make your contribution a great one?!

Write About It: You're Here for a Reason

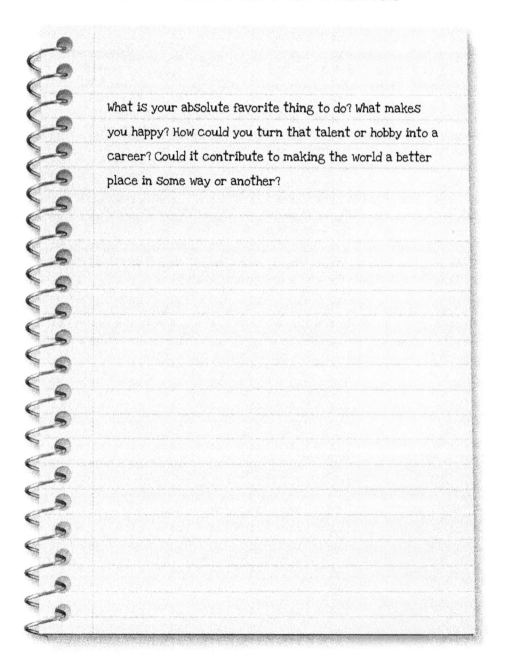

What is your absolute favorite thing to do? What makes
you happy? How could you turn that talent or hobby into a
career? Could it contribute to making the world a better
place in some way or another?

Chapter 4. Creating Great Character

"Personal success is built on the foundation of character, and character is the result of hundreds and hundreds of choices you may make that gradually turn who you are at any given moment into who you want to be. If that decision-making process is not present, you'll still be somebody—you'll still be alive—but you may have a personality rather than a character, and to me that's something very different.

Character isn't something you were born with and can't change, like your fingerprints. It's something you must take responsibility for forming. You build character by how you respond to what happens in your life, whether it's winning every game, losing every game...or dealing with hard times.

You build character from certain qualities that you must create and diligently nurture within yourself, just like you would plant and water a seed or gather wood to build a campfire. You've got to look for those things in your heart and in your gut. You've got to chisel away in order to find them, just like chiseling away rock to create the sculpture that previously existed only in the imagination.

"Watch your thoughts, for they become words. Watch your words, for they become actions. Watch your actions, for they become habits. Watch your habits, for they become character. Watch your character, for it becomes your destiny."

—Frank Outlaw

But the really amazing thing about character is that, if you're sincerely committed to making yourself into the person you want to be, you'll not only create those qualities, you'll strengthen them and re-create them in abundance, even as you're drawing on them every day of your life. That's why building your character is vital to becoming all you can be."

—*Jim Rohn,* author of *Leading an Inspired Life*

As teens, what makes our life seem so unbalanced or unsteady? You know what I'm talking about, right? That feeling we all get sometimes where it's like our whole world is literally crumbling to pieces. Sometimes we feel like we are given *way* more than we can handle, and it's normal to feel stressed and overwhelmed. Whenever I hear adults say that teens have it sooooo easy, I feel like saying "Uhmm, excuse me? Since when has being a teenager been a piece of cake?!" How about *never*?! Sure, most teens don't exactly have bills to pay, or families to take care of, but we have plenty of other responsibilities to worry about!

While growing up, everything about our lives seems to be constantly changing, and it's like we never know what's going to happen next. One day our best friend seems amazing, and the next day, we wonder why we were ever even friends in the first place. School seems to be going great, until someone makes fun of us or ruins our day and makes us want to crawl into a hole and never come out. The jeans we spent our entire paycheck on are the "turn heads" trend one week, but the next week, they're on the what-not-to-wear-list. Our parents are cool, until, of course, they find every single way possible to embarrass us (well that's just what it seems like sometimes).

The styles, opinions, and people we build our lives around are *always* changing, and trying to keep up is not easy by any means. Have you ever felt like you had no one to count on? Have you felt completely overwhelmed, on the verge of just wanting to give up? Have you ever felt like nothing you do is good enough? Good, me too. I think everyone has felt that way at some point. The constant turbulence of a teenager's life is really tough sometimes, but there is one thing you can do to make it better. There's one thing you have complete control over, and one person you can *always* count on. That person is **you**.

"Character is higher than intellect."

—Ralph Waldo Emerson

There is no doubt that teens live very busy, active lives filled with school, sports, work, family, friends, drama (which is sometimes just inevitable), boyfriends, girlfriends, clubs…and the list goes on and on, and on. It's hard to balance everything because after all, we're not perfect. It all seems so hectic because those are things that are always changing; things that we don't always have control over. We can't control whether or not our entire team will give it their all and play their best in the championship game, we can't stop our parents from getting divorced or our teachers from giving us unnecessary amounts of homework, and we can't control whether or not someone loves us. Those things just happen on their own. They do their own thing, despite what we want sometimes.

Since we can't always control those things, it's important to center our lives around what we *do* have control of. That's where our attitude, morals, and character come in! Oftentimes, the people, ideas, or groups that we commonly "revolve" around aren't *constants*, but are instead *variables*. Many of us can relate these terms to our often very boring math classes, but hey, our teachers aren't completely wrong about applying math to real life, because in this case, we most definitely can.

"The time is always right to do what is right."

—Martin Luther King, Jr.

So what exactly are variables and constants? Variables are people, things, or ways of life that change. **Variables** are constantly coming in and out of life's equations. Friends, school, hobbies, sports, relationships…those are all variables. We can't always control them. But **constants** are things that we know will always be there. Constants are our **character traits**. No matter what equation we're dealing with in life, and no matter what changes we go through, our character will always be there. Always. We decide how to react to situations, how to treat other people, and ultimately, the type of person we want to be, and how we live our life.

As long as our focus in life is set on building our character, and as long as we stick to who we truly are, the other points in our life will be easy to deal with. You are you! No one and nothing else is you, they're just factors in the wholeness of who you are. Relationships, school, sports, hobbies…those may impact who you are, but your *character* is ultimately what you're made of! Create yourself to be happy and confident with traits that will *never* leave you as long as you build them and apply them to your life. Building good character leads to guaranteed success, because *you* control it. Some awesome character traits include…

- ☐ **Integrity**—Create your own great character and stay true to who you are!

- ☐ **Honesty**—Be truthful with yourself and others.

- ☐ **Respect**—Show consideration for yourself and others. Always.

- [ ] **Responsibility**—Know what your responsibilities are and take action on them!

- [ ] **Caring**—Help others in need, and take good care of yourself.

- [ ] **Appreciation**—Be thankful for what you have, and give back.

- [ ] **Courage**—Don't be afraid to be the amazing person that you know you are. Don't ever doubt yourself. And don't let anybody else make you doubt yourself.

- [ ] **Leadership**—Set a great example and be a role model to those around you.

- [ ] **Patience**—Understand that some things just take time, and that's ok.

> "A life lived with integrity—even if it lacks the trappings of fame and fortune is a shining star in whose light others may follow in the years to come."
>
> –Denis Waitley

- [ ] **Wisdom**—Yearn to learn more and open your eyes to everything around you. Soak it all in, and gain knowledge. You will grow as a person, and become wiser.

- [ ] **Confidence**—Know that you are great and that you can do whatever you set your mind to.

- [ ] **Perseverance**—Have the strength to keep moving, even when you feel like giving up.

Character traits are the stuff we're made of! And what's so awesome is that *we* decide which traits will define us. So…if you want to be the best person you can be, pick character traits that will help you do that. Each day, think about what traits you're made of, and whether or not you're truly living up to them! Apply them to your life, and they will become habits. They will become a huge part of you. Build great character, and by doing that, you're creating a better *you*!

Write About It: Creating Great Character

What are your strongest character traits? What are your weakest? How can you improve at each trait and become stronger in that area?

Chapter 5. Finding Time to Chill

"If you don't know yourself and don't take time for yourself, then you can't have a good relationship with yourself. It's so important to figure out what makes you happy."

—Peyton, Age 19

When I was younger I'd sit around with my dad while he watched the news. I'd ask him questions about everything I saw. I've always admired how smart he is, and it seems like no matter what I ask him, he has an answer—like an encyclopedia. Sometimes I feel like he just knows everything (even though I don't always want to admit that haha). Considering all the endless and hectic things going on in the world, I've always been impressed with how he was able to keep up to date with every current event out there! You name it, he knows it. While watching the news as a little kid, I remember being so confused, not really sure what certain stuff meant. I'd tell my dad, "Gosh this world is crazy! I really don't want to grow up, because I don't want to have to worry about all of these confusing things—taxes, bills, war, politics—the stressful things about being an adult!" But he'd simply say "It's ok Bec, it's not so bad...you just have to make time to do the things in life that you love to do...find time for yourself and relaxation! Then it won't be so stressful. Work hard, but play hard too. Always remember that!" Call me Peter Pan, but I just wanted to stay young forever. How cool would that be, right?! Where your decisions consist of which cereal to eat that morning, and which bedtime story you want to read at night; not which credit card to use to pay the bills with, or which type of health care you need.

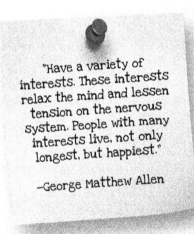

"Have a variety of interests. These interests relax the mind and lessen tension on the nervous system. People with many interests live, not only longest, but happiest."

–George Matthew Allen

Back then, I didn't want to think about growing up. But now, time has flown by, and I'm not a little kid anymore. So much for staying young forever—that didn't really work. Now, I understand what goes on in the world (for the most part) and reality has hit. And sometimes, that's pretty stressful. All the responsibilities that come along with age just keep piling up. I'm sure you guys know what I mean. Even though we're not completely adults yet, we still have SOOO much to worry about every single day. Whether it's grades, relationships, having to help support your family, trying to find a way to go to college, or just trying to figure out who you are, growing up has plenty of stressful things that come along with it. But now I totally understand what my dad meant by "work hard, play hard." We may not have careers and families yet, but we still have work and responsibilities like school, jobs, sports, or taking care of our family. We work just like adults do, it's just in a different way…but what's important is that we don't let that stress us out. That's where playing hard comes into the picture…

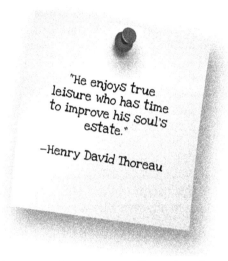

"He enjoys true leisure who has time to improve his soul's estate."

–Henry David Thoreau

Even though at times it feels like there is too much on our plate to handle, we just have to sit back and find time to relax and take time for ourselves. So what do I mean by "work hard, play hard?" Well, I mean that yes, of course we still need to do the things we need to do, and take care of our responsibilities, but we can't let those things define our life. It's so important to find time for ourselves, time to reflect, time to think, time to relax, and time to rejuvenate from the stressful things that go on in our lives. On the news, or in magazines, adults talk about ways to "de-stress," or ways to "relax and rejuvenate." But what about teens? Don't forget that we need to do that too! (Hey, we could even use nap time in school—just like in kindergarten—wouldn't that be nice?!)

So, how do we do that?!

Here are some simple ways to put the stresses of life aside and get in touch with our inner selves, and our inner-happiness!

Take time to think about your day

This may sound like an obvious statement, or something that we just do automatically every day, but it's deeper than that. Do you really take time to sit down and write down everything you did that day and then analyze it? Of course not…we shouldn't feel the need to do that, and who really has time for that? Even though we don't sit around and write novels about our lives, it's important to take at least a minute each night and just think about our day. Think about what you did, where you went, who you were with. Think about your actions, and your emotions. Is there anything you would've done differently? Probably, and that's cool because we can learn something new about ourselves every single day. Reflect on what you liked and didn't like and what you learned. This sounds so simple, but it's honestly difficult to do sometimes, because it seems like we're always in a rush, or just going day by day by day and not really taking the time to look back. I agree that the past is the past, but it's also how we learn and grow as people. When we take time to think about our day, we're taking time to improve who we are.

"Sometimes the most important thing in a whole day is the rest we take between two deep breaths."

–Etty Hillesum

Find something you love, and go do it

For a lot of people, their way of rejuvenating includes doing something that makes them happy, that takes their mind off of the hustle and bustle of daily responsibilities. Here are some… but what are yours?

- ☐ Exercising and playing sports

- ☐ Doing art

- ☐ Playing music

- ☐ Shopping

- ☐ Dancing

- ☐ Cooking

- ☐ Meditating

- ☐ Praying

- ☐ Spending time in nature (my favorite!)

- ☐ Writing (stories, journaling, poetry, songs...)

- ☐ Sleep (now that's one we all love ☺)

No matter what it is you love to do, whether it's in that list or not, make sure that you give yourself time to do that… take a break from hard work, and play hard! Life isn't supposed to be stressful, it's supposed to be enjoyable. We **all** deserve that, and we owe it to ourselves, so make sure that you're allowing time for yourself and time to just be—just be here, be who you are, and be doing what you love. Chill often. It's feels amazzzzzing!

"Peace. It does not mean to be in a place where there is no noise, trouble, or hard work. It means to be in the midst of those things and still be calm in your heart."

—Anonymous

Write About It: Finding Time to Chill

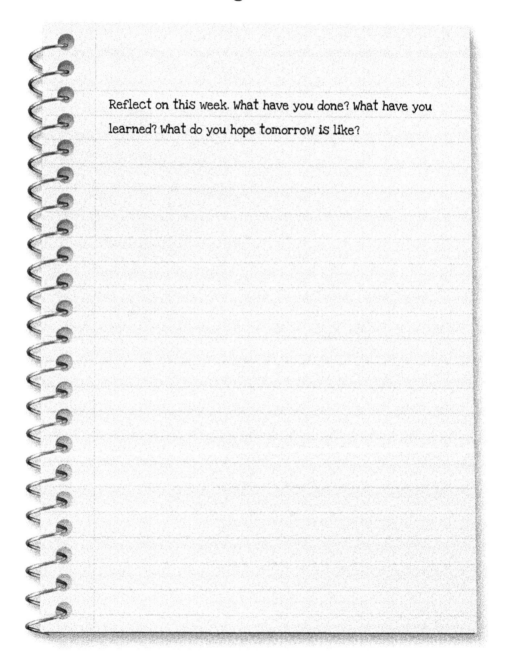

Reflect on this week. What have you done? What have you learned? What do you hope tomorrow is like?

Chapter 6. Building Strong Relationships

"The ability to build and sustain healthy relationships as a young adult is integral in the pursuit of a successful life. In many ways, the people we hang out with and have relationships with not only help shape our thoughts, worldview, and beliefs, they also contribute to our very character."

—*Maddi, Age 17*

This year, my family and I went to Florida for Christmas and New Years. I was all excited about leaving the freezing cold snow covered mountains of North Carolina to visit the warm and welcoming Sunshine State. The trip didn't really turn out how I thought it would though. To start out, on the day we were supposed to leave for Florida, we got snowed in at our house on top of the mountain. There was about a foot and a half of snow, and getting down two miles of our icy mountain road didn't look too promising. But we shoveled as much snow as we could, made it down the icy mountain, and we were finally on our way!

"Some people come into our lives and leave footprints on our hearts, and we are never the same again."

—Flavia Weedn

Then, on our way back home from Florida, we were in Middle-of-Nowhere, South Carolina. The alternator light came on in our car and we knew that wasn't good. How were we going to make it back to North Carolina with a dying battery!? Not to mention, it was New Years weekend and no auto part stores were even open. Once the car battery died, we had to give up on our attempt to make it home that day. With no juice left in the car, my dad barely made it off the exit ramp into a hotel parking lot. Right when we pulled in, the car completely stalled. The next morning, we met a sweet old lady named Deloris, who saved the day.

She worked at the hotel, and when she heard about our situation, she immediately offered to give us a ride into town. Of course, we accepted. ☺ She drove my dad and me to the store, and we bought a new battery and the tools that we needed. We were just so thankful Deloris helped us out. After hours of working in the freezing cold, my dad fixed the car! We were able to get back on the road, and head towards home. We said goodbye to Deloris and thanked her several times. We knew if it wasn't for her, we would've been stuck there for a while. Finally driving away, not feeling stranded anymore, I thought about Deloris and how people like her are more important in our lives than we think. It was amazing how someone was sooo ready and willing to help out complete strangers!! She was just a visitor in my life, and although my family and I will never see her or talk to her again, I won't forget Deloris or her act of kindness.

"Strangers are just family you have yet to meet."

–The Five People You Meet in Heaven

Usually when we hear the word "relationship," we think of boyfriends, girlfriends, and Facebook relationship statuses. But there's so much more to that word than it seems. Obviously, we aren't *in* relationships with everyone, but we can *have* relationships with just about anyone—our parents, friends, teachers, siblings, the lady in the checkout line at the grocery store, the hotel lady who gives you a ride when your car breaks down, or the guy who sits next to you in biology. We can learn something from just about anyone. From Deloris, I learned that it's great to do something for people in need, even if they are strangers to you. You see, we don't necessarily realize it now, but the people we meet throughout our lives help make us who we are. So why not invest some time and interest into not only the people who seem to be with us through every milestone in our life (the regulars) but also all the random, yet meaningful people (visitors) we meet along the way?

Regulars are the people who come into our life regularly and stay for a while. It makes sense that they'd be called regulars, right? These people could be parents, teachers, close friends, or maybe for some people, God. Our relationships with them are the most important. They're like frequent flyers on our flight to Adulthood. They deserve to be treated well. In order to ensure that, good communication and a strong relationship are really important. As I said earlier, these people help create us, and leave huge impacts. Good relationships with our regulars are nice, and something many of us have already accomplished, but **great** relationships are even better, and something everyone can work on.

The second type of person is the visitor. These people could be acquaintances or people we only see once and then never again, like Deloris. Everyone has people like this. Every day at school, we walk past tons of people, and the chance that we're friends with every single one of them is pretty slim. But, you know those people that you see over and over? The people you've talked to maybe once in the lunch line, or maybe sit next to in one of your classes. Those are visitors. It may not seem like it, but we have relationships with them, too!

The relationships we have with the people in our lives (both regulars and visitors) are awesome, unless something goes wrong. Drama, fights, arguments, and misunderstandings are things we all experience at one point or another. So what should we do when a relationship gets flipped upside down? Well, the most important thing to do is have a good attitude about it, and remember that things get better in time. At our age, the most common relationship fallouts happen between boyfriends and girlfriends, but they also happen with friends and family.

"There are big ships and small ships, but the best ship is friendship."

–Anonymous

First we'll talk about **boyfriends, girlfriends, and break-ups**. At our age, boyfriends or girlfriends can seem like everything. For some teens, that's what their entire world revolves around. The bad part about that is that if you make someone your "everything," then you end up with *nothing* if you lose them. That's why it's so important to remember not to get too caught up in a relationship. We're still young, and although it's fun to date people, we don't have to be so serious about it right now. We still have the rest of our lives to figure out who we want to be with. Of course there are those sweet, yet rare stories of high-school sweethearts (like my parents), but most of the time, teenage relationships are sort of like a roller coaster. One day everything could be perfect, and then the next day it's over. Let's take a look at 16-year-old Erica's story about dealing with a breakup from a two-year relationship…

I was in a rough relationship for 2 years with a boy that I fell head over heels for. I loved him and his family so much. I even thought that this was the boy who I would spend the rest of my life with, and would never be able to live without. He treated me like an angel and we couldn't be happier. But eventually, things just started to go downhill; we were arguing over stuff that didn't matter at all! I thought, "Hey this happens in a lot of relationships. We'll just have to work through this." But I unexpectedly got a call from him one day, telling me that I deserved much better. After a night of tears and frustration, I realized that I had been through a lot to keep this boy in my life and I had let him treat me however he wanted, because I was never strong enough to let him go. Towards the end of our conversation, I realized that there was nothing more I could do; this was the end. I had to accept the fact that a friendship was our best way to go. Months later, we are still friends, still have that same love for each other, and always have each others' backs. My friends and family have helped me keep my head up and be the strong girl that I know I can be. I still cry every now and then when I come across that song of ours, or the many pictures scattered around. But I don't regret any moment spent with him. I know my decision was one of the hardest, but it was also one of the best.

—*Erica, Age 16*

Sometimes letting go of someone else is the best thing you can do for *yourself.* Yes, it feels awesome to have that special someone, but we shouldn't let them define who we are, or make them the center of our lives. Erica mentioned in her story that she let her boyfriend treat her however he wanted to, because she wasn't strong enough to let him go. She got attached to him, which is something that happens to a lot of teens. Break-ups aren't fun, but when they happen, we just have to step back and look at the big picture. Our boyfriend or girlfriend is not what makes us who we are. We are our own person. *We* make ourselves who we are. So when relationships don't work out, remember that it's not the end of the world. Although it may feel like part of you is missing, you're still there, and you're still you. Look at break-ups as a chance to start fresh. Spend time with friends, and do things to get your mind off it. Do what you love, and focus on yourself. Don't dwell on it or let yourself get depressed. Rise above the situation, and never allow a break-up to control your life. Because whether or not we think so at the time, life will go on, and things *will* get better with time ☺

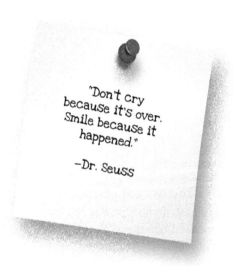

"Don't cry because it's over. Smile because it happened."

–Dr. Seuss

Break-ups aren't the only tough things we have to deal with, though. Issues with friends and family happen, too! Drama, jealousy, arguments, misunderstandings, and fights are all things we wish we could avoid. But sometimes they just happen. Just as with break-ups, when we have issues with friends, or our siblings, or our parents, it's important to have a good attitude and rise above it. Be the bigger person. Don't let someone else totally ruin your mood—you're better than that. Sometimes people hurt us, or make us mad, and sometimes we do the same to them. It's life. We're all guilty of making mistakes, and if we do make a mistake, one of the greatest things we can do is be brave enough to apologize. Sometimes we just have to suck up our pride, and take the higher road by saying "I'm sorry." And when you apologize, you would want your friend to accept your apology, right? So when people apologize to you, be strong enough to accept genuine apologies. It doesn't necessarily mean that what they did is ok, or that you're just going to forget about it. It takes a very strong person to be able to forgive and be able to accept apologies. But know that you can do

"Sometimes you just have to forget what you want, and remember what you deserve."

—Anonymous

it. Life is just too dang short to hold grudges against people. Make the most out of every relationship by having love, forgiveness, good communication, a positive attitude, and plenty of respect. Relationships are like a plant. They need to be cared for properly, or else they'll wilt. So how exactly do we do that? Well, here are some simple ways to build and strengthen relationships:

Build Relationships Up: Meet new people—Being comfortable and confident enough to meet new people is the start of creating a new relationship. There are plenty of opportunities to make new friends or meet someone new, and when you take advantage of that, it feels really good. You can learn a lot from someone else, and you can make people feel really good by showing that you care.

- ☐ If there's a new kid at school, offer to sit with them at lunch. Introduce them to your friends.

- ☐ At parties or gatherings, don't be afraid to introduce yourself or talk to someone you've never talked to before.

- ☐ Organize a "mix it up day" at your school during lunch where everyone has to sit with people they don't know very well.

- Get a group of friends together and organize a pen pal group with teens from another country! Keep up with them online or through mail and get to know their culture.

- Join a volunteer or service club or organization in your town that allows you to meet people whom you wouldn't have met otherwise.

- Become part of a community activity like co-ed sports teams or church groups.

- Try to open up your mind and be more accepting of people who are different from you. It's amazing what you can learn and how much fun you can have with someone who's completely different from you!

"Make new friends but keep the old, Some are silver and others are gold."

–Girl Scouts Motto

Keep Relationships Strong: Show appreciation for the people you care about—Of course it's always great to meet new people and make new friends, but it's also really important to keep those relationships that you already have, and make them stronger. Let friends and family know that you care about them by showing appreciation—even if it's in a small way.

- Make a card or letter for a parent or sibling or close friend just to say "thanks" for being there for you. It may sound cheesy but a "thank you" can go a LONG way!

- Plan to spend a day with someone you wish you spent more time with, like your mom or dad, or brother or sister, or maybe a grandparent. Sometimes we get so caught up with our friends, and school, and sports, that it's easy to forget to show our families appreciation. Spending time with them is really the best gift you can give.

- Make a phone call to a close friend that you haven't talked to in a while. Give yourself time to just catch up and hear about what's new in their life.

- Communicate. A lot of times arguments with friends or family happen because there was a miscommunication or a lack of communication (or drama! We've all been there, dealt with that.) If you're having an issue with someone, talk to them. Don't just keep it bottled up—that will only make things worse. Communication is key.

☐ Be there for them. When our friends or people we care about come to us with tough situations, a lot of times we don't have the right words to say. But that's ok because what can mean so much is just a listening ear. Be there with open ears, even if you know you don't have the answer to their problem.

Obvious or subtle, relationships are there with everyone who walks into our lives. We can take the opportunity to learn something from everyone we meet, and better ourselves and the people around us. I like something that Mother Theresa said... "Let no one ever come to you without leaving better and happier." That's an awesome thing to remember. Whether someone is a regular, or a visitor, do what you can to make a positive impact on them, and open yourself to them and learn from them. Even if it just means sharing a smile, or saying hello. Small things can make a big difference! Relationships are what life is made of, so build them, and build them strong ☺

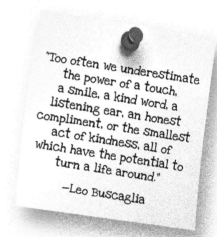

"Too often we underestimate the power of a touch, a smile, a kind word, a listening ear, an honest compliment, or the smallest act of kindness, all of which have the potential to turn a life around."

–Leo Buscaglia

Write About It: Building Strong Relationships

Think about somebody who has positively influenced your life. Write them a thank-you note or letter. Then, write down some ways you think you've influenced someone else's life.

Chapter 7. R-E-S-P-E-C-T

The other day on Facebook, I saw a fan page called "I learned how to spell R-e-s-p-e-c-t from Aretha Franklin." I thought that was pretty funny. Obviously knowing how to spell *respect* is something we learn at a young age, whether we learn it in school, or from Aretha haha. But when do we actually start to understand its meaning? I'm sure we'd all like to believe that we've always known what it means, and we also probably like to think of ourselves as respectful people. But are we really? Do we really know what it means, and do we show respect as often as we should?

There are different types of respect—respecting yourself, respecting the environment, respecting others—but in this chapter, we're going to focus on respecting others. In the very first chapter I talked about loving and respecting yourself and how important it is to be able to do that. But besides respecting yourself, it's important to respect others. *Obviously* this is something that we've heard all throughout our lives. The "Golden Rule" and treating others the way you want to be treated are words we hear from the very beginning. We know what it means, and we know it's important. But, it's not always easy to be respectful, especially when people say or do things that make us really mad! (Which can happen quite often…) But going back to the golden rule, it really does make a whole lot of sense. No one wants to be treated badly, made fun of, or walked all over. We know that we don't want that for

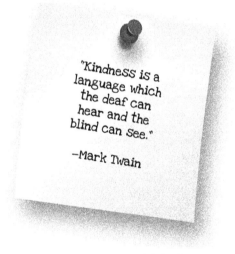

"Kindness is a language which the deaf can hear and the blind can see."

–Mark Twain

ourselves, so we shouldn't bring that upon other people either. Think about well-respected people. What is one thing they usually all have in common? They show respect for others! It's an age-old virtue that will never go out of style. What's sooo awesome about respect is that it totally has the whole win-win thing going on. When you respect other people, you make them feel better, and you feel better about yourself!

Try to think about a time when someone was really mean to you. Think back far…maybe even to elementary school. Come on, we *all* have times where we've been disrespected. So think of one or two, or many specific times, and try to remember what it felt like. Now wait, why do you still have those memories, especially if it's from a long time ago? Why have those thoughts stuck with you all this time? You have that memory of what happened and how you felt because it was a time that affected you. It's something you may never forget because you were hurt, mad, or upset all because of someone else. So why would you ever want to be the person who hurts someone else? You wouldn't, right? (Well, at least I hope not haha).

Now, think of a time or multiple times when someone did something nice for you and it completely turned your day around, or your life around. Feels good, huh? It feels really good. It's awesome when people go out of their way to be respectful to you. It makes you feel important, makes you feel like you matter, and makes you feel better about yourself. And it most likely made the person who was nice to you feel good too. That goes back to the win-win thing. You can't really lose with respect on your side. So we may not want to be the disrespectful people from our memories, but we can **all** strive to be the respectful ones!

At our age, respect is something that definitely seems hard to come by. Teens can be so mean and hurtful to parents, teachers, siblings, friends, and especially each other! But why is that? Why is there SO much gossip, SO much bullying, SO much hatred?! It's ridiculous. It really is. Those are the things that lead to low self-esteem, depression, or feelings of worthlessness, which no one should ever have to experience! It can even lead to something unbelievably sad—teen suicide. Teen suicide is one of the leading causes of teen deaths. I mean seriously, how terrible is that!? Teen bullying is completely **un**acceptable and NEEDS to stop *now*! **No one** should ever, ever, ever feel so low that they wish to take their own life. That's one of the reasons respect is so important—you never know when your words and actions can completely change someone's entire life! So let's try to get to the bottom of this—right here, right now.

Suicide is a permanent solution to a temporary problem! If you or someone close to you has thoughts of suicide, or to answer any questions you may have about teen suicide, visit www.suicidepreventionlifeline.org or The American Foundation for Suicide Prevention at www.afsp.org!

When people are disrespectful, it could be because of several different reasons. Let's think about the different types of disrespectful people, and then we can get a better look at how NOT to be ☺ Maybe you know some people like this… and hey, since none of us is perfect, maybe we're even guilty of fitting the characteristics of these people at one point or another…

First, there's

☐ **The nonchalant**—This type of person has a personality where nothing they say or do affects them, and they don't mind if they hurt anyone else. Maybe they could also be titled somewhat heartless (or is that way too harsh?)

Then, there's

☐ **The legitimate**—This type of person says or does something disrespectful in order to defend or stick up for him or herself. In some cases, that's really important. You never want to let people walk all over you! But there are other ways to deal with that too, which we'll talk about later. So, the **legitimate** may actually have a good reason to react, but maybe ends up taking it a little too far.

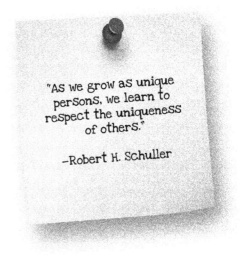

"As we grow as unique persons, we learn to respect the uniqueness of others."

–Robert H. Schuller

And there's

☐ **The careless**—This type of person says and does things on impulse, without really thinking about how it would make someone else feel. They don't necessarily mean to cause problems, but they sometimes forget to think before they act or speak. (ooops)

But don't forget

☐ **The wannabe**—This type of person is disrespectful JUST because they think they need to be in order to "fit in." They say or do what they *think* would be considered "cool." They don't fully realize that by being mean, they're obviously not being cool. The two just don't go hand in hand.

And finally there's

☐ **The green-eyed-monster**—Yep, you guessed it... this type of person is just plain jealous. This is probably the most common type of disrespectful person when it comes to GIRLS. The green-eyed-monster type enjoys being mean because it actually makes them feel better. By putting others down, they get a *temporary* feeling of accomplishment and contentment. We all know that's the way to go... NOT. It's obvious that jealousy happens...a lot. Probably more often at our age than any. But being mean to others to try to feel better? Not exactly the best solution.

So as I said earlier, I'm sure we're all guilty of acting like one of those types at some point or another...I know I am. But what's important now, is that we learn from who we've been before, and decide who we want to create ourself to be for our future. Hopefully we all want futures full of happiness and fun, and being respectful to ourselves and others can lead us there. These five types of traps of disrespect are easy to fall into, and hard to get out of. The most important thing to remember in order to avoid being the "disrespectful person" is to truly think before you act and speak, and think about how your actions affect the people around you.

"I don't have to attend every argument I'm invited to."

—Anonymous

So what can these different types of people do to turn disrespect into respect? Well...

The **nonchalant** should care more about other people's feelings and think about how their actions would affect someone else.

The **legitimate** should remember to be kind to others even when others aren't kind to them. We should NEVER let people walk all over us. That would be disrespectful to ourselves, but we have to find that balance. Don't be a doormat, but don't take it too far! Find balance between those. The middle ground consists of being the bigger person, so show that you're not going to stoop down to that lower level of immature words and actions.

The **careless** should stop to truly think about what they are doing or saying and how they'll make someone feel. Most importantly, they need to think before they act.

The **wannabe** should finally realize that being disrespectful isn't cool! It's awesome to be able to set a good example, and you should always stand up for people who are being picked on. Never feel like you have to be disrespectful in order to sound cool.

The **green-eyed monsters** should stop and think about their actions, and think about other people's emotions. They need to stop taking their jealousy out on others by putting others down just to bring themselves up.

There are two extremes to feeling good about yourself:

1. **You can put others down to *temporarily* make yourself feel better (short-term happiness)**

2. **You can be respectful, lift others up and *definitely* feel better about yourself (long-term happiness)**

I think we can both agree that long-term happiness sounds a lot more exciting, so we might as well make that happen! The point is, if we have ever acted in a way we shouldn't have towards someone else, we can make improvements, and we can bring disrespect to an end. There are so many other ways to deal with emotions, but taking them out on other people just isn't the answer. I think we all know that by now, but sometimes we just…forget. Honestly, if we think before we act or speak, we won't really have a reason to have regrets. If we want to become better people, striving to be respectful throughout every opportunity we have is essential!

"Kindness is more than deeds. It is an attitude, an expression, a look, a touch. It is anything that lifts another person."

–Anonymous

Well, we all know what respect is, but when it comes to applying it to life, it's not always easy for everyone. If you want to be a well-respected person, then you have to respect others. That leads to our next point—it's the little things you do that make a difference. So here are some quick ideas on how to achieve win-win happiness…

✓ If someone is clearly having a bad day, say something nice to make them feel better. Compliments are awesome, but only as long as they're honest compliments. Be sincere. Don't make up stuff just to sound nice.

✓ Even if someone isn't having a bad day, you can still say something nice. Even when you feel good, you can always feel better.

✓ Do random acts of kindness. When opportunities to be respectful pop up in front of you, act on them. Go out of your way to do something nice for someone else.

✓ The best acts of kindness are those that no one even sees you do. Even if you know that no one will ever know you did it, do something kind anyway.

✓ If you see someone sitting alone at lunch, offer to sit with them.

✓ If there's a new kid at school, become their friend. Don't be afraid to meet new people.

✓ Say "Thank you." Simple words like that make a world of difference.

✓ Stick up for people. If you hear your friends or other people picking on someone else, don't be afraid to change the subject, or say "Hey, that's not cool."

"For more information about bullying, visit www.teensagainstbullying.org or www.stopcyberbullying.org"

✓ Don't ever be a cyberbully. Comments or remarks on Facebook, MySpace, or any other online network can be seen by anyone. It's the same with texting. Things said online or through texts are just as hurtful as things said in person. Help our generation put cyberbullying behind us!!!

✓ Take the higher road. If someone does something that hurts you or makes you mad, don't let it bring you down, and don't react negatively to it. Fighting back may make it worse. Show that you're stronger than that by just ignoring it and moving on.

✓ Kill people with kindness. Well, don't actually kill them, of course haha. But even if people are mean to you, be nice back. They'll be impressed by how you're able to handle the situation in such a mature way!

✓ Make it a promise to yourself that you won't join in on conversations where someone is being made fun of. Be the bigger person, and vow to think before you speak.

✓ Stick to *your* character. Don't let others influence you into being disrespectful. Have the confidence to do what you know is right.

✓ Be a leader and a role model for others. Set a good example for those around you, by being the most respectful person you can be.

Respect isn't something that we're born with, and it isn't always easy to show respect—that's for sure. Especially when you feel like someone doesn't deserve it. But do it anyway! Be kind anyway! Isn't it great to know that by simply being respectful, you can make a positive difference in someone else's life, and your own life too? Showing respect should be a no-brainer. Make it a habit!!! I know sometimes it seems difficult, but it's not as hard as it seems. It takes about 21 days for something to become a habit. If you make it a point to be respectful as much as possible, it will become a way of life for you. You will notice a difference, and the people around you will too!

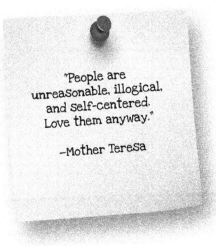

"People are unreasonable, illogical, and self-centered. Love them anyway."

–Mother Teresa

Write About It: R-E-S-P-E-C-T

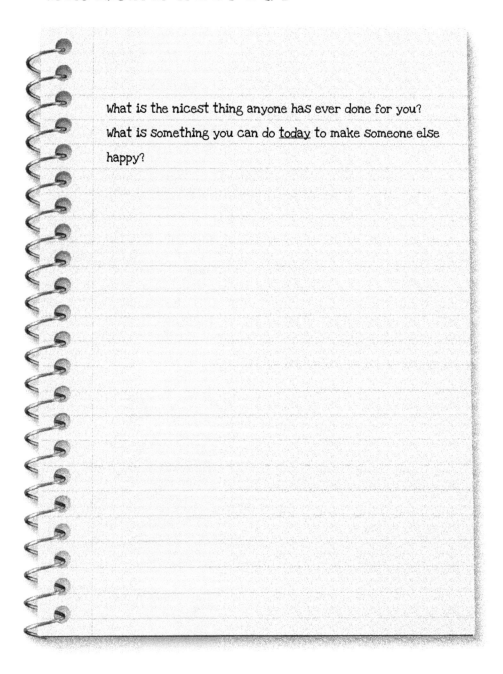

What is the nicest thing anyone has ever done for you? What is something you can do <u>today</u> to make someone else happy?

Chapter 8. The Art of Acceptance

"Understanding other people's differences and accepting them makes your quality of life better. Getting to know those who are different from you, and taking the opportunity to learn from them, makes you a truly remarkable person."

—John, Age 18

What do you think of when you hear the word *acceptance*? What does it mean to you? I sat here for a while trying to figure out how to exactly define acceptance. I kept typing up sentences, and then deleting them. But none of my attempted definitions seemed to honor the word with its proper meaning. It's a tough word to define, because it's heavy, touchy, and carries a *whole* lot of meaning. It can mean so many different things—acceptance of people, cultures, ideas, situations, opinions... or even having to accept disappointing sports stats, bad test grades, or your dad's out-of-date clothing...yep, acceptance applies to pretty much anything. Although it can have a multitude of meanings and references, there is one thing that can be said about acceptance—it is very powerful. All throughout our lives we are faced with chances to either accept or well, unaccept. (Is that even a word? Haha) A lot of times when things or people are different from us, or if ideas or opinions aren't the same as our own, it's hard to understand how to tolerate them. But that tolerance is so important, because when we learn to accept the things in our life that we may not always have control over, we give ourselves the chance to see so many awesome things about this world!

"Happiness can exist only in acceptance."

–George Orwell

Especially at our age, and probably at any age really, we are faced with so much pressure, a lot of tough situations, and *many* opportunities to form opinions. Sure you may be thinking "But I'm me, I like being different, I have my own views and opinions, and I don't want to agree with everyone else." And that's a great position to have! You should never feel like you have to agree with the people around you on every little thing, but there is a huge difference between agreeing and accepting. If everyone in the world agreed on everything, this world would be completely boring. I mean everyone would be so much alike, and there would be no diversity. The fact that people don't agree on everything is *great*, because it makes people unique. It only becomes a problem when people can't agree to disagree. That's where acceptance comes into play. We obviously won't always agree on others' thoughts and opinions, and we may not even agree with situations we're faced with. But if we can accept the differences, and know that those differences are what make the world great, then we're able to have such an awesome appreciation for this diverse world around us.

So let's think about us for a second. Let's think about people *our* age. What are some things that we have the choice to either accept or "unaccept?"

- ☐ Ourselves

- ☐ Family

- ☐ Environment

- ☐ Culture

- ☐ Society

- ☐ Tough Situations

First we'll talk about ourselves—A lot of times when we think of "acceptance," accepting ourselves isn't exactly the first thing that pops into our head. We usually think about accepting people who are different from us. But before we're able to do that, we have to be content with ourselves. Accepting yourself goes hand in hand with loving yourself, just like we talked about in the first chapter. You'll never get anywhere in life if you aren't happy with who **you** are, and you'll never be completely happy without first accepting yourself. So what kinds of things should we accept about ourselves? Well, things we can't change of course. If there's something we don't like about ourselves, like our attitude for example, that is something we can change and improve. But what about the things that are harder to change? Like stuff with our body, or the way we fit in, or our talents and abilities. Not everyone is going to have the so-called "picture perfect body."(Actually, scratch that, because there is no such thing as a picture-perfect body anyway haha!). Not everyone is going to be liked by everyone and fit into every crowd. And not everyone is going to be an Olympic gymnast, or a pro basketball player, or a famous pop star. But that's all okay, because no one is perfect. If there are things you don't like about yourself, and they can't be changed, turn it around and learn to love them.

I used to have a pretty big gap in between my two front teeth, and I absolutely hated it. I thought I looked so ugly, because all my friends had "pretty" teeth, and everyone on TV had "pretty" teeth, and I wanted to have "pretty" teeth, too. I wanted braces so badly so I could get rid of that gap! My parents always told me it didn't matter if I had a gap or not; inside I was still the same old Becca. They liked my gap. They thought it was cute. I didn't agree. So I got braces, and today, I'm gap free. But looking back now, I see exactly what my parents meant. My gap was something that made me stand out, something that made me unique, something that made me different. Instead of trying to get rid of it, I could've learned to love it! (And my parents would've saved a whole lot of money). Now, I see tons of models in magazines with gaps, and I really admire how they never changed that about themselves. They accepted something about themselves that was different, and learned to love it, and even ended up modeling! That gap didn't stop them. So even though that's a really small example of accepting yourself, my point is that the things we may not like about ourselves that make us different are actually really great. And instead of wanting to be different, or wishing to change, we should embrace who we are! You're the only YOU out there, so keep it that way!

"If you don't like something, change it. If you can't change it, change your attitude."

–Maya Angelou

16-year-old Matt understands the obstacles that may come along when dealing with self-acceptance. In his inspiring story, he shows us that we should never be afraid to be ourselves! He also shows us why it's so important to accept our peers and the people around us. Check it out...

"The highest courage is to dare to appear to be what one is;" John Lancaster Spalding, a famous Catholic Bishop and author once said this, and I can't agree with him more. Ever since I was little I always thought I was different from the other kids on the playground. This is probably because I am different. I am a gay man. To some, this may seem to be a very trivial issue that I've had to overcome, but having grown up in a small town with strict conservative parents and many overly-conservative peers, accepting myself was hard. For most people, accepting themself for who they are in being gay is one of the hardest things to do and many never accomplish this. But I didn't want that kind of life. I wanted to be who I was no matter what that person may be as long as in the end I was happy. Sure I could fake dating girls; maybe even get married to

one and fall in love with their character and not their physicality. But should I have to? No. Everyone is entitled to their own happiness and should be able to be anyone that they believe they are meant to be.

Everywhere I ever lived when I was younger had an anti-gay presence to it. My elementary school experience was horrible. Teasing was only the first part—having no friends because of my insecure shyness that was stemming from my differences was the hardest part. Even at a young age, I knew that one day, I would have to admit to myself what I was and move on, and that was a challenge in itself. I believe the first step towards being comfortable with one's homosexuality is acknowledgment. I had to acknowledge myself for who I really was, or forever live a lie and be unhappy and awkward. I remember saying to myself "I'm gay" after feeling miserable one day when I came home from middle school. That day, someone at school said that I "talked like a faggot." Puberty hit and my voice deepened—drastically—to the point where I would say "hey" in the hallways and people would mock me for having such a deep voice. But this didn't hide the fact that deep inside I still hid a dark secret that could have possibly ruined my whole reputation. I never really came off as the "gay" type either; I always had many guy friends (post- elementary school), and I had normal boy interests. I suppose this is why when I "came out" during my sophomore year in high school, no one really believed me, and some still don't.

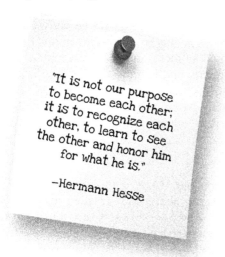

'It is not our purpose to become each other; it is to recognize each other, to learn to see the other and honor him for what he is."

–Hermann Hesse

I believe this to be the hardest obstacle I had to come across because it was really hard; the gossip was harrowing. For about a week that's all anyone would ever talk about. I got over it and so did they, and in the end no one cared. I set the example—for many gay men in my school who were in the closet or "finding themselves"—that it's okay to be gay. I also broke many stereotypes and showed that being gay isn't about wearing pink, talking with a lisp, and having a favorite Cher song. It's about being who you really are and showing bravery, which is something that a lot of people can't do. Being gay is a battle that I still fight with. Acknowledgment is too easily compared to accepting oneself, and that is the other part to being comfortable with one's homosexuality. I still fight with this today and I will forever do so until I become victorious and quit caring what other people think. But at least I can say I overcame part of the gigantic mountain that many never even try to climb. If someone doesn't accept you, you should never feel hurt, because you shouldn't have to change who you are just to suit the needs of someone else.

—*Matt, Age 16*

Matt had to accept who he was in order to be able to fully live his life. He couldn't allow the opinions of others to stop him from being the person he knew he was. Matt's story is an inspiration because he was courageous enough to be different and loves himself for who he is.

Family—What's your family like? Who are the people you consider family? Parents? Siblings? Grandparents? Aunts? Uncles? Cousins? Friends? What do they mean to you? Think about those three questions for a second. I'm sure many of you have terrific families and could go on and on saying wonderful things about who they are and what they mean to you. And that's so awesome! Because it's true that family is so important! But a lot of times, we have some things about our families that we wish we could change. Maybe your little brother is super annoying, or maybe you don't get along with your dad, or maybe you think your mom is crazy. Or maybe tough stuff has happened in your family that has really impacted your life. Teens are stuck in hard situations ALL the time! It's really hard, because on top of all the other things we have to deal with, family shouldn't be one of them. We should be able to have that place we can come home to and feel relaxed. But that's definitely not always the case. Parents get divorced, people pass away, people move out, people argue, people abuse…so many tough things can happen within in a family, and a lot of times, we have no control over it at all. That's where acceptance of family comes into play. To everything from accepting the fact that your mom may not be "cool," to dealing with a parent going to jail… things happen; every day, all the time, to every family. And it's never easy. And it's not always something we agree with. But when we allow ourselves to accept the things we can't change, we help free ourselves from disappointment, sadness or anger.

Environment—This can mean a few different things. Our environment can include the place where we live, the school we go to, or the people we're surrounded by. How many of you got to decide where you're living today? Probably none. Maybe a couple, and if that's the case, you're extremely lucky, because at this age, we pretty much have no say in what city or state we live in, or even what school we go to. When I was in elementary school, my family and I moved from Connecticut to North Carolina. I didn't really mind. I was excited to leave the city and move to the mountains. But I was also really young, so that's probably why I didn't mind. I think it was a lot different for my older brother though. He was in middle school, that time in your life where being the new kid is totally NOT easy. But he didn't have a choice. He had to pack all of his things just like the rest of us, and move from the North to the South. It was a big change for him, and looking back now, if I were him, I never would've wanted to move—having to leave all of his friends, and his school, and the place where he grew up. But he had a good attitude about it, and accepted it. He knew that this environmental change was something he didn't have any say in, and so he moved and made the most of it. We can't always choose where we are or who or what we're surrounded by, but we can choose our attitudes and the ability to accept things we can't change.

Culture/Society—Wow! Where to begin?! Take a second to think of things in society that you agree with. Maybe you associate with a certain religion or a political view, or opinions on world events. Having an opinion on these

"Acceptance and tolerance and forgiveness—those are life-altering lessons."

—Jessica Lange

things is important. But now, think of things that you disagree with. Chances are, there are probably more things you disagree with than agree with haha. But that's because everyone's different and we all have our own views. Now let's take a second to apply this whole "acceptance of culture" thing to our lives. Let's narrow it down to the people around us—our friends, our peers, our teachers—are there things about them that you agree and disagree on? I'm sure there are. Maybe you like country music, and the kid who sits next to you in English likes rap. Or maybe you're Jewish, and your teacher is Christian. Maybe you're black, and your partner for your science project is white. Maybe you're straight, and your best friend is gay. Or maybe you're democratic, and your neighbor is republican. These differences in opinions, race, ideas, and interests are *everywhere*! We're constantly either agreeing or disagreeing with people on things. It's one thing to disagree and have your own opinion, but it's another to take it to the next level and judge someone because they're different from you in one way or another. When you learn to accept the differences around you, you grow *so* much as a person!

"I think everyone has something to offer and everyone can learn from someone else if they allow themselves to. I've realized one of the most important things in life is living with open ears, an open mind, and most importantly, an open heart. Not that you shouldn't censor the things you tell certain people, and the type of people you let in, but everyone deserves a chance. Had I not taken chances on building friendships with people, I wouldn't be where I am today, and I wouldn't have learned all that I have."

—Ellie, Age 18

Like I've said over and over, diversity is so awesome. When you accept that, you're opening your mind to infinite opportunities. Even though we're all different, we're all people, with feelings, emotions, and opinions each of our own. Learning and growing as a person begins with acceptance.

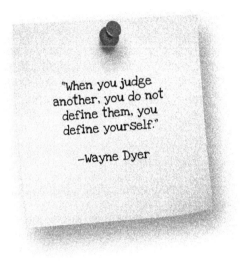

"When you judge another, you do not define them, you define yourself."

—Wayne Dyer

Tough Situations—I touched on this a little bit earlier, when I talked about tough situations with family. Those happen a lot, to a lot of teens. But tough situations aren't just at home. They're at school, work, with friends, or with ourselves… tough situations show up all the time. Maybe you didn't get accepted into the college you wanted, or maybe you got fired from your job, maybe your boyfriend or girlfriend broke up with you, or maybe your best friend broke a promise. Things like this aren't fun to deal with, but once something happens, it can't be reversed. Sometimes it's best to just accept the tough things that you cannot change. I used to make a big deal out of things that I couldn't go back and change, but my mom and dad always said "Sometimes you'll just have to roll with the punches, Bec." Now I know exactly what they meant by that. You may or may not be the prayerful type, but acceptance reminds me of a famous and thoughtful prayer…

"God, grant me the serenity
to accept the things I cannot change;
the courage to change the things I can;
and the wisdom to know the difference."

—Reinhold Niebuhr

It is so true. If you want to change something to become a better person, and if you are able to, go do it. But if you're not in control, learn to accept it. Life will be much more fulfilling and much more rewarding if you do.

When I was in 8th grade, we went on a school trip to Atlanta, and I must admit, it was pretty awesome! I remember at one point, we visited the church that Martin Luther King, Jr. went to. There, a bubbly old man gave a quick inspirational talk to us 8th graders, and there's one thing he said that has stuck with me. He talked about how it's important to be like a sponge. (Not Spongebob, just…a sponge). He told us to take every opportunity we can to soak up the information and knowledge around us. The more we soak up, the more there is to us…the more of a person we become. When we accept, we are doing two things

1. Living with the things we cannot change, tolerating them, and making the most out of it

2. Opening our eyes, mind, and heart to the world around us.

Of course it's important to stand up for what you believe in and have your own opinions—diversity is what makes the world great—but it's also important to soak up as much as you can and accept and embrace diversity!

Write About It: The Art of Acceptance

What does the word "acceptance" mean to you?

Chapter 9. It's <u>Your</u> Body

*"It's simple, really. You're lucky. You're lucky because you're alive. And being alive means you get to enjoy all the wonderful things that this world has to offer. Your body is what allows you to live. So, how can you **not** be thankful for it? How is it possible to **not** love your body?"*

—*Emily-Anne, age 16*

Ever noticed how different everyone looks? Of course you have! Sure there are some people who look similar, but no one is exactly the same. (Even identical twins are unique in some way.) Brown hair, blonde hair, black hair, red hair… dark skin, light skin, tan skin, pale skin…brown eyes, blue eyes, green eyes, hazel eyes…tall, short, fat, thin, young, old…there are endless ways to describe the way someone looks. How do you describe yourself? When you look in the mirror, what do you see? What you see in that mirror is unlike anything anyone else sees when they look in the mirror. Because there really is *no one* else on earth who looks exactly like you! Think about that. I think that's really cool. No matter who you are, there is no one else who has ever lived or ever will live who is just like you. You are your very own person.

So often as teens, we feel like we *have* to look a certain way—like there is only *one* look that is perfect and acceptable, and we try to mold ourselves to fit that image. But that's completely unnecessary. Stick thin, big boobs, blonde hair, long toned legs—tall, dark, handsome, muscular—sure, those are fine looks for some people, and if you're one of those people, that's cool. But not everyone has that look, and that's totally ok. Just because it's in a magazine, or on some "reality" TV show, doesn't mean that it's the *only* way to look. If everyone tried to follow those cookie-cutter images, what would this world come to? Let's just say that it would be lame. So instead of trying to be someone else, or trying to look like someone you're not, focus on the things that actually make you, you. Just as we talked about in the last chapter, there are things we can accept about ourselves so that we can love our bodies more! Being unique is awesome!

What makes your appearance unique?

☐ Your clothing

☐ Your hair

☐ Your eyes

☐ Your skin color

- ☐ Your height

- ☐ Your weight

- ☐ Your race

- ☐ Your age

- ☐ Your gender....and the list could go on and on and on...

Our whole lives we are told to love ourselves and be happy with the way we look. But we know that's much easier said than done.

I mean of course we all have things we don't like about our appearance. It's just human nature. So let's do a quick activity. Take a minute and become *whoever* you want to be. How exciting haha! In the left box (The True You) draw what you actually look like, and in the right box (The Dream You) draw the "new you" or what you would change about yourself if you could... I'll do it too! This activity confirmed the fact that I am *horrible* at drawing people haha. So if you're anything like me, and can't draw, just use words to describe.

The True You   The Dream You

Now maybe the "you" in both drawings looks the same, because maybe you're already happy with how you look, and you don't want to change anything. If that's the case with you, that's so awesome! Keep it up! You are lucky that you can be happy with yourself for who you are! ☺

If you actually drew (or described) two different people, let's think about *why* you did that...

Like we all know, it's human nature to sometimes want to look different or change something about our appearance. That's why we may cut and dye hair, buy new clothes, or wear makeup. Changes are great, and people like to feel good about the way they look. But look at the two drawings. What did you change from the first one to the second one? Different hair type, longer legs, more muscular arms, no freckles, thinner stomach, no gap between your teeth (haha remember that?) Why did you change the things you changed? Are you truly unhappy enough with something that you would want to change it forever? Well, now look at the two drawings and compare them. Do they even look like the same person? If you wished to change a bunch of things about yourself, you wouldn't even be the same person anymore. The things that you may not love about yourself are often the things that make you unique, and make you who you are. Sure there are some things that are fun (and healthy) to change—it's fun to change your hair color, and it's healthy to exercise to tone up your body... but if you get to a point where you're not happy with who you are, or if you become obsessed with the way you look, that's never any good. If there's something you don't like about yourself (maybe big ears, or small eyes, or teeth that aren't perfect) take them and turn them around into something that makes you different, and love it! Take what you used to hate, and turn it into something that you'll promise to embrace about yourself.

"They cannot take away our self-respect if we do not give it to them."

–Mahatma Ghandhi

So, now that we discussed some things we don't like about ourselves, let's think of what we love! We *all* have some great things about our body! What are yours? When you can find things to love about your body, you gain **self-confidence**! So what exactly is it and where does it come from? Well, self-confidence is our ability to be happy with ourselves. When it comes to our body, self-confidence is knowing that you are you, and that is good enough for yourself! It's not always easy to be confident, especially when there are people everywhere who influence how you view yourself. Many teens deal with low self-esteem and low self-confidence because of always worrying what others think. This can lead to depression, a negative attitude, self-abuse, or even eating disorders. That's why being happy with who YOU are, is essential to being happy in any other area of your life. Let's take a look at Devin's inspiring story about overcoming her battle with an eating disorder, and we'll see how she learned to love herself for who she really is...

Ever since I was younger, tracing all the way back to the fourth grade, I've been worried about my weight. Now, being a freshman in college, I realize how completely and utterly disgusting this is. I was in elementary school and worrying about whether or not I was "fat." I started acting on these insecure thoughts—"Am I fat? Am I attractive? Do I need to lose weight?"—when I was in eighth grade. When high school came, things just got worse. My method of maintaining control of my body was exercise. Exercise would make me thinner and keep me thin. The worst part of it all was that I was nowhere near being fat. The most I weighed in high school was 104 pounds. At the peak of my eating disorder, I weighed less than 95 pounds.

For the first sixteen years of my life I lived in a small, rich town in New York. Looks were everything. If you were hot, you got attention. If you weren't, guys didn't bother with you. Why should they when they could have the hot girls? At least this is the way I saw life in this town. Throughout my pre-teen and teenage years I felt like I was constantly compared to my best friend. I always had this secret hatred for her, for the fact that in everyone's eyes she was perfect. She was tall, thin, had huge boobs, and was gorgeous. The problem was, it wasn't her fault that I was jealous. In fact, she was the

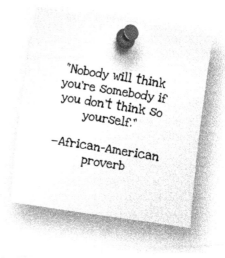

"Nobody will think you're Somebody if you don't think So yourSelf."

–African-American proverb

one person who was always there for me, always believed in me, and always thought I was beautiful on the inside and out. The worst part was that it wasn't strangers who would compare us everyday. It was my other best friends. Over the years I've tried to suppress the memories and statements people made to me. The one thing that will never be suppressed is how each comparison made me feel. Being compared to someone, especially someone who makes you feel belittled is the absolute shi**iest feeling in the world. I felt worthless and hopeless. I was miserable. I would sit and watch as my best friend was praised *for everything and I was shoved to the side. Little statements suggesting I was nothing compared to her would set my self-esteem at a lower rate every day.*

Running changed it all. It was my safe haven, or so I thought. It wasn't until my freshman year, though, that I started running. Running took my eating disorder to an extreme without me even realizing it. Looking back now, I recognize many reasons for this. Running was something I was good at. For once, people envied me for something. Running was also an escape. As I ran, I ran from the remarks, the comparisons, and the lack of perfection in my life. As cheesy as it sounds, running was the best natural high. It managed to momentarily take away all of my issues, only to make things worse when I was done.

Running wasn't only something I could control, but it controlled me as well. My obsession with running turned into an obsession with exercise. And when I say exercise, I mean exercising all day, everyday. My daily schedule consisted of waking up thirty minutes early to do ab workouts. I'd eat a sandwich bag full of cheerios at school, plain with no milk. (Milk would make my stomach expand and make me look "fat.") After successfully eating every last cheerio in my sandwich bag, I'd sneak into the girls room and do pushups. I'd go to class. I'd eat lunch. I'd go to the bathroom and do pushups. I'd get out of school. I'd go to track practice and run an average of three to five miles a day. I'd go home and do more ab workouts. I'd eat dinner. I'd do MORE ab workouts. I'd eat dessert. I'd do more ab workouts. I'd go to sleep. The next day would be the same exact routine. After everything I ate, no matter how small or how big, I'd have to sneak off and do ab routines. The problem was, I knew I was sneaking around to do them. I continued with these habits for the four years throughout high school.

At the time, I didn't think of it as an eating disorder. Looking back I realize I had an eating disorder called exercise-induced anorexia. Overall, I had this eating disorder for five years! During these five years, I was completely miserable. I would constantly look down at my stomach, making sure I wasn't getting fat. I would only eat certain foods and only at certain times of the day. I would look at myself in the mirror and cry. I would stand there staring at myself, looking myself in the eyes and just get hysterical. I couldn't believe how hideous I was; how absolutely ugly I was. I was disgusted with myself and I didn't know how to change it. I couldn't control my face, so instead, I controlled my stomach. Each time I'd go to the doctor, my weight would continuously go down. I started out weighing 104 pounds in high school. It disgusts me to think that when I eventually weighed 94 pounds I was extremely happy. I couldn't hold back the smile when I saw the small number on the scale.

Then, when I was sixteen years old, I was involved with a guy. I refused to have sex with him because I knew I didn't want to have sex until I was in love. It started out as flirting. It turned into him being the guy I had all my first sexual experiences with (other than actual sex). However, me being a naive tenth grader, I completely ignored the fact that he was "hooking up" with someone else as well. His attention would shift between the two of us. I was the secret girl, though. He paid me no attention in public. I'd watch as the two of them would go upstairs to mess around. Once she left for college that summer, all the attention shifted back to me. He suddenly wanted to give me attention in public. More importantly, he loved to brag about how good I was when we fooled around. It didn't dawn on me until years later that these were insults, not compliments. I vowed from this point on to make guys prove to me I was worth something; not just a girl to do sexual stuff with. To him, that's all it was—a casual summer hook-up. To me, he was the epitome of the person who made me hate the person I was, and made me struggle with an eating disorder.

This was easy to do because the summer after my eighth grade year, I moved thousands of miles away to North Carolina. My best friends were distressed over the idea of this. Me, on the other hand, I couldn't wait to start over, get away, and escape all the a**holes who were secretly ruining my life.

I truly believe starting over completely saved my life. In North Carolina, I met someone who completely changed my life: Andrew. He was the first person who I admitted my eating disorder to. I don't know exactly when it was that I realized I had an eating disorder. I eventually got to the point where I was exhausted. I couldn't physically nor mentally handle it. The day I told Andrew about my issue was the day my life changed. I was able to open up to him because despite everything, he loved me. He encouraged me to conquer my biggest fear and admit my eating disorder to my mom. I was terrified of disappointing my mom. However, the biggest weight was lifted off my shoulders. Everything was going to turn around.

*I didn't just snap out of it, though. Recovering from an eating disorder has been the most struggling battle of my life. Even after admitting to having one, I still continued to worry about my image and weight. Eventually, Andrew suggested therapy. I've been in therapy for over a year now and it has been the most amazing experience of my life. The person I am today is completely different from the person I was for the past five years. Today, when I look at myself in the mirror I do not cry. A smile stretches across my face as I recognize the fact that I am beautiful and sexy. I recognize that I am Devin. The world around me does not define who Devin is. The only person that does is **me**. As long as I look at myself with positive thoughts and recognize the beautiful person I am, then the rest of the world will too. That's when my life changed; when I learned* *that the only person that needs to see the beauty in me is **me**. It isn't easy. Some days are really good while others are really hard. Every day is still a battle, but every day I constantly remind myself of who I am and how far I've come. Every day I look myself in the eye and tell myself I'm beautiful. And the best part of it all is I believe myself.*

—Devin, Age 19

If you or someone close to you is struggling with an eating disorder, know that there is help available! Eating disorders are very serious, and no one should ever have to feel like they're alone. For more information, visit NationalEatingDisorders.org or call their Helpline at 800-931-2237

Like many teens do, Devin got to a point where she felt really unhappy with her appearance and the way others saw her. That issue with appearance not only affected her physically, but emotionally too! By worrying about the way she looked, she risked her health. Devin was so brave to admit to herself, and others, that she had an eating disorder. That takes SO much courage to do! And by doing that, she was able to get help and support and overcome the disorder that had taken over who she truly was deep down. Devin is a perfect example of how sometimes, as a teen, we get to really low points in our lives and feel ugly, or worthless, or not good enough. She is an inspiration to other teens because she shows that to turn around that negativity, all we have to do is realize that we are all physically unique, and there is no such thing as "that perfect body" or "that flawless face." We are who we are, and we need to love and accept the way we look. We are all different, and when we allow ourselves to truly believe that, we are able to live a much more wholesome life!

Celebrities, the media, peers, friends, boyfriends and girlfriends, parents… they all affect the way we see ourselves. The most important thing to remember is that no one else can *make* you feel a certain way about your body. Sure they can influence your opinions, but it is *you* who ultimately decides how you feel about your appearance. If people talk crap, ignore them. If people compliment you, take it to heart and use it to remind yourself that your body is fine the way it is.

So how do you stay self-confident? Remind yourself every day of the things you love about yourself. Every time you look in the mirror, don't try to find flaws! That's stupid! Why would you want to remind yourself of something you don't like!? Instead, look at what's great, look at what you love! Appreciate you, because there's only one in the world.

Aside from being happy with your body and your appearance, **taking care of your body** is just as important! When your car's motor is shot, you can fix it. If a house burns down, it can be rebuilt. When a friendship falls apart, it can be mended, but when a body isn't taken care of, you can't just go out and buy a new one. This is YOUR body and YOUR life; you only have one body, so make it last! What can you do to stay happy and healthy? These are things we hear all the time, but it's all important to remember!

Eat Right—Make sure that you're eating the right *amounts and types* of food that are right for your body!

☐ Ever wanted to know exactly what types of food are right for *your* body? Are portion sizes a little confusing to you? Visit **mypyramid. gov** to create a personal food plan for yourself based on age, weight, height, and physical activity! You can also track your progress, and get helpful tips!

☐ Eat breakfast every morning (even though we all know it can be easy to skip, especially when we're in a hurry!) Even if it's just a granola bar and a piece of fruit, eat something so you start out your day right. It's the most important meal of the day! Oh, and *don't* skip meals! Did you know skipping meals can actually cause you to gain more weight? So try to eat three healthy meals per day. You'll look better and feel better!

☐ When you're given the chance to choose between different food items, choose the healthiest ones. Yes of course it's tempting to choose the double-chocolate ice cream sundae over the fruit salad dessert, but even the smallest healthy decisions like that one can benefit your body. And don't be afraid to try new foods!!

☐ Work on healthy eating habits! Just like everything else we've talked about in this book, creating healthy eating habits takes time. If you already have healthy habits, way to go. Keep it up! But if not, right *now* is the time to start thinking about how you can make your body even healthier, because everyBODY deserves to be happy!

☐ Encourage your family to eat healthier too! That way, everyone's on board to achieve a healthier lifestyle. Don't keep so many tempting junk food snacks in the pantry. Try to stock your kitchen with nutritious items for everyone to enjoy. It's easier to eat healthy when you completely eliminate unhealthy choices!

☐ Stick to the plan! If you make a promise to yourself to eat healthier, don't break that promise. Sure it's tempting to make exceptions at times, but don't fall behind on your goals. After a while, eating healthier will become completely natural, and you won't even *want* to eat junk food anymore!

Exercise often—We all know how important it is to exercise, but sometimes it's hard to find the motivation to actually do it! But we have to, because it's an essential ingredient to staying happy and healthy!

☐ Is it hard for you to commit to workouts? (It definitely is hard for me sometimes!) If so, try partnering up! Find a friend or a family member to exercise with. That way you both hold each other accountable, and it makes exercise a *whole* lot more fun!

☐ Make a plan for yourself. Come up with certain activities or exercises to do on certain days of the week. Try to work out at least 3 days per week—even if it's just for 30 minutes at a time!

☐ Set goals for yourself! Wouldn't it be awesome if we could just work out one time, snap our fingers, and then magically see amazing results?! Yeah of course it would be great, but sadly it doesn't happen like that. But that's why goals are so helpful. When we set goals for exercising, we have a *purpose* behind what we're doing, and that makes the effort *so* much more worth it! When you actually have to work hard for something, it means a whole lot more in the end!

☐ Remind yourself of why you're exercising, and remember your purpose for doing it. Keep your goals in mind and know that even if you don't see immediate changes, you are still doing something great for your body! (*Just don't over-do it. Too much exercise can be dangerous.*)

☐ Don't slack off! If you set a plan for yourself, don't quit. Keep moving forward. Of course there will be days where you'd rather lounge around on the couch, or sit at your desk Facebook-stalking... but exercise is important. So make it a regular part of your life.

☐ Make it fun! Exercising and working out isn't supposed to be some unbearable and horrible experience. It's supposed to make you feel better. So by making your physical activity fun, it doesn't even feel like a workout. One of my favorite workouts is simply blaring music in my bedroom and dancing around. It's movement, it's fun, and it breaks a sweat! Find a form of exercise that's *fun* for you. Try aerobics, or yoga, or a sport you've never done before! Trying something new can be a lot of fun ☺

"To keep the body in good health is a duty... otherwise we shall not be able to keep our mind strong and clear."

–Buddha

Make smart choices—One of the greatest things about being a teenager, is that we're given so many choices. All of those choices are opportunities to learn and grow and become the best people we can be. Many of the choices we make in our lives now, affect the choices we make later on. So it's important to make sure that we're living a life full of choices that we're *happy* with!

At our age, we are constantly faced with decisions about alcohol, drugs, sex, and more! And sometimes those decisions can be really tough! We may feel like, at the time, it's the right thing, or the cool thing to do, and then later on totally regret the choice we made. That's why it's so important to THINK before we ACT! In this story from 19-year-old Jennifer, she shows how NOT thinking before you act can lead to something you completely regret. Just this one decision about sex completely changed the way she views her body, and the choices she *now* makes.

Recently, I experienced a life-changing moment that gave me a new perspective on the way I view myself and relationships. I was on vacation with my family and a friend. We were at a hotel on the beach—talk about the best getaway ever! One evening, we met up with family friends for dinner at this restaurant that was a little while down the street from the hotel. It was right on the water with tables outside and volleyball courts lining the restaurant. My friend and I would take the younger kids out to the water to play in the sand, to keep them occupied while we waited for our food. I'd go back and forth with them to the water, passing the tables that were outside.

There were two guys at one of the tables that I kept seeing as I walked to the water. One of them was a cutie and I smiled at him a few times. He reciprocated and eventually waved me over to say "Hi." I turned to my friend and she smiled and said, "Go on." As I walked over, all that was rushing through my head was, "How do I look? What are they thinking? I hope they're nice." The guy that was smiling at me introduced himself and asked me how old I was. Both guys were shocked at how young I was and thought that the kids I was watching were my own. I looked at the pitcher of beer between them and thought they had to be a little buzzed. I thought to myself: "So they've got to be over 21; that's fine, right?" I asked them what they were doing later, hoping that there was something exciting to do, and they said they were probably going to hang out at the restaurant and play some ping-pong. That seemed like a harmless hangout, so we exchanged numbers and I went back to my table.

I told my friend everything and she got excited, because we didn't want to just hang out in the hotel room and do nothing. After dinner we walked back to the hotel and were getting excited for our night ahead. Little did I know what was about to come. I heard my phone go off and felt a rush of tingles go through my body. I told the guy that my friend and I were ready and he responded, "I just want to hang out with you." This gave me mixed feelings because I didn't want to leave my friend but I really wanted to go out and do something fun. I told my friend that I wanted to go out and she understood. She wanted to stay in the hotel anyways but just told me to be careful. That was the first red flag...but it didn't seem like a problem to me at the time.

So I met the guy half-way between the hotel and the restaurant. He walked over to me and gave me a huge hug and I could smell beer and cigarettes all over him...second red flag. He started walking in the opposite direction of the restaurant and I said, "Aren't we going to play ping-pong at the restaurant?"

If you've been sexually assaulted or raped, or if you're unsure as to what is considered sexual assault or rape, visit www.rainn.org or call 1-800-656-HOPE for free, confidential help.

His response was "Nah, let's take a walk on the beach." At the time, that statement seemed harmless so I nodded and followed. We walked for a while and then sat down looking at the water. He turned his face to me and started kissing me. I was a little shocked but thought that everything was fine; this was ok. Well, I was wrong.

He undid his pants and then mine. I kept saying "no," and that I wasn't ready, but he ignored me. He said it would be really quick. You would think the next thing I would do is kick him where it hurts and run back to the hotel, but I was in such shock I didn't have time to think of that. All I could say was, "Do you have a condom?" I figured I had better be safe than sorry. It felt like the longest night of my life. Afterwards, I went back to the hotel and was beside myself. How did I let that happen? Why was I so stupid to go off by myself with a stranger? These questions were flying through my head like a rocket. I was so confused and worried; I thought I made a big mistake. The next morning I debated telling my friend everything that happened. I was so embarrassed, but I stuck up my chin and told her. She was quite pissed. She kept saying, "Why didn't you push him off? I can't believe you just did that!" I tried to tell her that it sounds so easy to just say "No," but once you're in that position it's much more difficult than it sounds.

"Though no one can go back and make a brand new start, anyone can start from now and make a brand new ending."

–Anonymous

The rest of the vacation was a drag and I had no idea what to tell my mom. We got back home and my friend and I weren't talking that much and I didn't know what to do. It took me a while, but I told a close friend of the family what happened and she said it was ok and that everything would be fine, but that I should tell my mom. That scared me. My mom and I are very close; she's like my best friend, but I couldn't bear to tell her this. After a month or so I fessed up and told her everything. She was mostly concerned with the fact that I went out at night with a stranger. I could have been kidnapped. This made it hard for her to trust me from then on but I told her I never wanted that to happen to me again. I blame myself for everything. I thought it was my fault everything happened. Yes I was naïve to go out at night with someone I barely knew but it wasn't my fault that he was on top of me.

Since then, I have been more concerned with my body and how I use it. I try not to regret what happened and look at it as a learning experience. I know now not to let a guy take control of me, or to put myself in a dangerous situation where there's no way I can get help. Just remember, you don't make mistakes, they are simply speed bumps that you learn from. Always trust yourself and never let other people force you into doing something you don't want to do.

—Jennifer, age 19

If Jennifer would've thought before she acted, she wouldn't have put herself in such a dangerous position. But that was something that she learned a whole lot from. It's something we can learn a lot from, too. Jennifer let her guard down, and just that one decision led to a night of regret. She's lucky that it wasn't worse. So many other things could've gone wrong. Thankfully, it was all okay in the end, but Jennifer's message is a strong one. We should *never* let other people make us do something we don't want to do—no matter what it is! Now I'm not your mom or dad, or any other adult. So I'm not here to tell you "don't do this, or don't do that." We've heard those words all our lives, so we don't really need to hear them again. We should get the point by now haha. But what I will say is this…

Visit AboveTheInfluence.com for more information about drugs and alcohol. Visit ItsYourSexLife.com for more info about sex!

*When it comes to drugs, or drinking, or sex, once we make the decision to do something, we can't take that back. We can't turn back time, or magically erase regrets. So simply think before you act. We both know what we should and shouldn't do. Don't do something just because it seems like everyone else is doing it. Never, ever, ever let anyone make you do something you don't want to do! Either you make the choices in your life, or someone else will make them for you. So **have the self-confidence to do what YOU know is right**. And really, really think before you make any decision. Think about yourself, and what you could be doing to harm your body, or negatively change your life forever. Just one bad choice—that's all it takes. Think about others and how your decisions affect them, or how you could seriously harm someone else. More importantly, **before you act, know the facts.***

When you *Live High on Life™*, you don't need drugs or alcohol to make you happy. Instead, you're able to create your own happiness in a healthy way. A lot of teens have trouble finding the self-confidence and courage to make decisions that are right for *them*. So think about it. Before you make any decisions, truly think about it…what is the life *you* want for *yourself?* **You decide.** Your body is a HUGE part of who you are. Love it, appreciate it, and most importantly, take care of it! That is *your* responsibility; so take control of your life and *love* who you are!

Write About It: It's <u>Your</u> Body

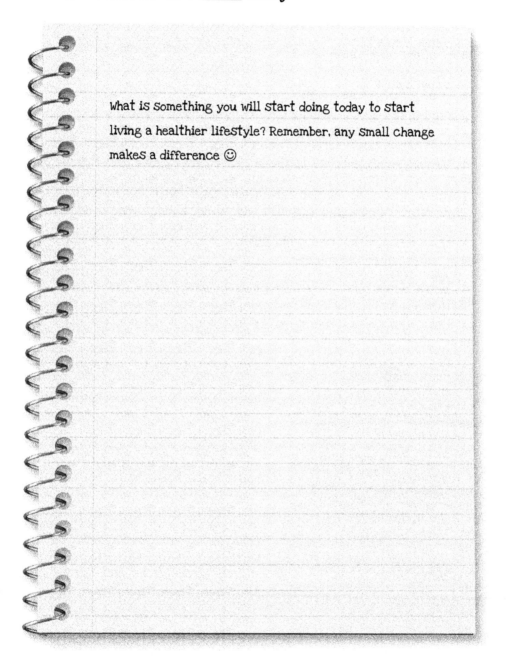

What is something you will start doing today to start living a healthier lifestyle? Remember, any small change makes a difference ☺

Chapter 10. Being a Green-Teen

"The Earth is not one single person's possession; it belongs to all of us. If we all make conscious efforts to positively affect our environment, it will make a huge difference for everyone."

—*Adam, Age 19*

The other day I was cleaning out my closet and I found a notebook full of stories I had written when I was little. The notebook was "creatively" labeled "Rebecca's Notebook of Short Stories," and was complete with many misspelled words and some hard to read handwriting. One story that I wrote was called *A Beautiful Place*. It definitely wasn't anything too impressive, but reading it made me think about our planet today and how things are changing. So, keeping in mind that this was written by someone with a 3rd grade level vocabulary and bad grammar, I welcome you to read the very, very, very short story, *A Beautiful Place*…

"Clunk, clunk, clunk" was the sound of a soda can blowing across the road. There was trash piled everywhere you turned in this little town called Dirtyville. (Again, aren't you just lovinggg the creativity here? haha) *Almost everyone that lived there would throw trash out their windows and litter.*

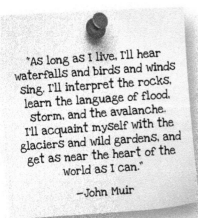

"As long as I live, I'll hear waterfalls and birds and winds sing. I'll interpret the rocks, learn the language of flood, storm, and the avalanche. I'll acquaint myself with the glaciers and wild gardens, and get as near the heart of the world as I can."

–John Muir

But there was one girl named Caitlin who never did any of that. Instead, she tried to clean it up. After three years of trying to clean it up, Caitlin realized that she wouldn't be able to do it by herself. One day, Caitlin came up with a club filled with people who would help clean up the mess. Caitlin wanted to name her club The Earth Savers!

As soon as possible, Caitlin posted as many signs as she could around Dirtyville. In two days, Caitlin had 13 people sign up. Time passed and that was still all the people she had. But Caitlin knew that 13 was better than 1.

The Earth Savers got together as often as possible. After more meetings, things got better and better. After a year The Earth Savers Club had done so great! Dirtyville wasn't dirty anymore. It looked beautiful and people liked it better that way. Now, not as many people litter there and I guess you could say that Dirtyville turned into a beautiful place!

Okay, so yes, I know that isn't the most entertaining thing to read, and I definitely can't say that it was well-written, but what I can say is that if I wrote something like that when I was seven years old, then obviously the Earth was something I cared a lot about back then. And that hasn't changed. I still love our Earth. I love nature and everything about it, and I work hard to respect and protect it just like many other people do. The reason I wanted to share that story with you, is because I wanted to make some quick comparisons. In that story, Caitlin sees that there's a problem in her town. People are harming the environment, and not realizing how bad it is. So, wanting to make a difference, Caitlin tries to find a way to help. So she starts the club, and together, they're able to go a long way.

"Study nature; love nature; stay close to nature. It will never fail you."

–Frank Lloyd Wright

The point here is that we all notice things around us that are bad for the environment (leaving lights on in empty rooms, keeping things plugged in when they don't need to be, throwing away recyclable materials, etc.). Even though we may think that as one person, we won't make an impact, that's not true! Because it takes just ONE person, like Caitlin, or like you, to spread awareness and set a good example. There's a huge difference between the impact that one person can have and the impact that 13 people can have. By doing your part, and letting others know how they can do their part, big changes are made! You may be thinking, "Duhhh I've heard all of this before," but even if this *is* common sense, obviously it hasn't hit everyone yet, because people are *still* being wasteful and irresponsible when it comes to our planet. And that has to change soon! *A Beautiful Place* was written through the eyes of a kid, but we're not kids anymore, so this is our time to step up our game and really take responsibility for caring about our one and only incredible home—our Earth. We're fully capable of caring, so why not start today? ☺

Well, where exactly can we start? For now, let's start with the basics.

What are the main issues?

- ☐ Global warming and climate change

- ☐ Ecological footprints that are way too big

- ☐ Habitat destruction and wildlife extinction

- ☐ Air, land, and water pollution

- ☐ Natural resources being wasted and destroyed

What's going to happen if it's not fixed?

- ☐ Animals (and people) will die

- ☐ Habitats will be ruined

- ☐ Water will be polluted

- ☐ Air won't be clean

- ☐ Our home won't be the same in the future unless we take responsible action TODAY!

"Live in the sunshine, swim the sea, drink the wild air."

–Ralph Waldo Emerson

This Earth is our home, and just like our body, we only have one. It is *our* responsibility to take care of it! Would you voluntarily destroy your own home? Heck no! So why harm the home that we *all* share? We need to realize the impact that we as humans have already made, and start working towards positive changes. Just like one person can make a difference, it's the little things we do that make a difference. A lot of times, we can make changes that are effortless…we just have to open our eyes to the world around us and see how we can do things to change our lifestyle to help the planet. What can you do to make a difference? What can we all do together? Well, it's actually easier than we think. The most important thing to remember is that every little change counts!

How can we help? Ever wanted a list of simple, fast, and fun ways to help the environment? Well, here you go!

- ✓ Recycle! Paper, plastic, aluminum cans, cardboard, glass...you know the drill. ☺

- ✓ Get a reusable water bottle instead of grabbing a disposable plastic bottle every time you want water.

- ✓ Set up a recycling box or bin in your room or somewhere in your house. That way, instead of *throwing away* old homework assignments, or love notes from your ex, you can conveniently recycle them!

- ✓ Find out about recycling pick-up in your neighborhood. If there isn't a pickup service available, bring your recyclables to a dropoff center.

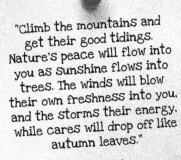

"Climb the mountains and get their good tidings. Nature's peace will flow into you as sunshine flows into trees. The winds will blow their own freshness into you, and the storms their energy, while cares will drop off like autumn leaves."

—John Muir

- ✓ Does your school recycle? If not, do something about it! Find out if they plan on starting a recycling program any time soon, or get a group of friends together and start your own school recycling program! You can apply for grants (like the Friends for Change grants through Disney) to help pay for recycling bins or compost tumblers.

- ✓ Start a "Green Club" or "Environmental Club" at your school or in your community. Get a group of friends together and come up with activities and projects to help give back to the earth! At my high school, we have something called "Green the Campus Day" where students and teachers come out to help clean up trash, plant flowers and trees, and help with yard work around the campus. And the best part is that it's actually tons of fun and feels good to give back!

- ✓ Read magazines? I know I sure do! (Esp. *Seventeen* ☺)What do you do with them when you're done? Sooo many magazines get swept away with the trash, but that needs to stop! Make sure you recycle yours when you're done, or donate them to a classroom that could use them for art projects or assignments! Or you could even make your own collage for your room before tossin' them into the recycling!

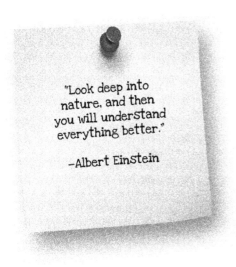

"Look deep into nature, and then you will understand everything better."

—Albert Einstein

✓ Unplug electronics that aren't being used. Did you know that even if they're not turned on, some still use energy just by being plugged in! Crazy, huh? So girls, unplug those hair dryers and straighteners, and guys, unplug those razors!

✓ Carpool, walk, run, or ride your bike whenever you can! You'll save gas, money, and eliminate that nasty auto pollution.

✓ Make sure you have a *full* load before washing dishes or clothes, or before drying clothes.

✓ Save *lots* of water by washing the dishes by hand instead of using the dishwasher.

✓ Hang your clothes out to dry when you can, rather than using the dryer.

✓ I know I'm definitely guilty of standing in front of the fridge *forever* trying to figure out what to eat, but keeping the fridge door open uses a lot of energy because when cold air is let out, the fridge has to work even harder to get cool again. So take a quick peek and pick a snack!

✓ Take shorter showers!! I know, I know, showers feel gooooood. But they can be such a waste of energy. Even cutting back by 2 minutes makes a difference! And take cooler showers! Did you know cooler showers use less energy?

✓ Change your light bulbs to energy-efficient ones (CFL bulbs).

✓ Find a small lamp for your room rather than using ceiling lights. And whenever you can, keep the lights off and open the windows to bring in *natural* lighting.

✓ Try composting! Instead of throwing away fruit or vegetable waste, or clippings from yard work, start a compost pile! That way, organic waste won't end up in landfills, but will instead get recycled naturally!

✓ Start a garden at your house. Grow your own fruits, veggies and herbs. You'll save money and eat healthier.

✓ Educate yourself on organic eating and farming and why it's so great! Find out where you can buy organic products in your town!

✓ Plant trees! Plant plants! They give off oxygen, and they are visually appealing. ☺

✓ Bring the outside in! Keep a plant or two in your room! Just make sure it's near a window where it gets plenty of sunlight! And don't forget, it doesn't rain in your room—so water your plants often. ☺

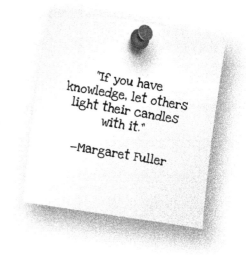

"If you have knowledge, let others light their candles with it."

–Margaret Fuller

✓ Volunteer at a National Park, nature conservancy, or wildlife habitat. You can give back while educating yourself at the same time.

✓ Be a summer camp counselor at an outdoor camp to share your appreciation for nature with younger kids! Be a role model and show them why it's important to care for the environment.

✓ Find out about internship or job opportunities in outdoor recreation or environmental conservation to help educate others on important issues.

✓ Spend time outside in nature to gain a better appreciation for it! That's right—leave your iPod and your cell behind, and step into the great outdoors! Really pay attention to what is out there—the sounds, the smells, the plants, the wildlife. Nature has an incredible way of providing rejuvenation and inspiration. ☺

✓ Yearn to Learn! Educate yourself, your friends, and your family! Remember, this is *your* responsibility because this planet is everyone's home!

Take Action.

☐ Don't just say you're going to help. Actually get up off your booty and make a difference!

Don't Stop!

☐ Keep learning more, continue giving back to the environment by being involved, stay up to date with environmental news, and teach others!

Visit the National Parks website at www.nps.gov to learn more about the National Parks or to find out ways to get involved! If you want to make a difference right now, *you can*! Visit **Disney's Friends for Change** at www. Disney.com/FriendsForChange for more tips and ideas on how to protect and care for our environment! Also be sure to check out more resources in the back of the book.

Write About It: Being a Green-Teen

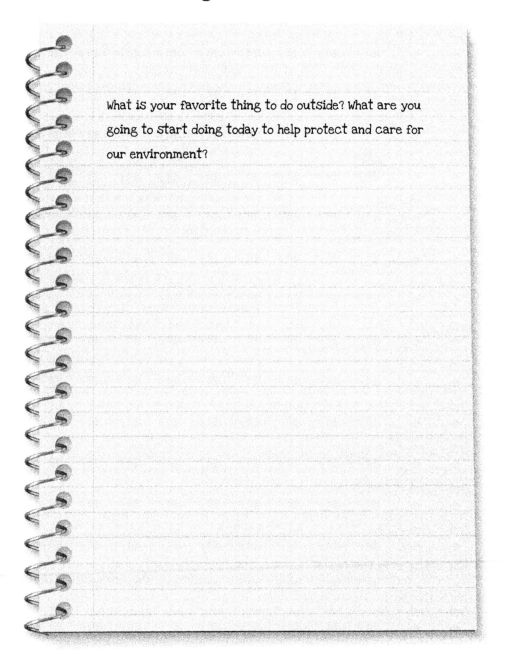

What is your favorite thing to do outside? What are you going to start doing today to help protect and care for our environment?

Chapter 11. Dreaming BIG and Setting Goals

"You need goals! That is how you will succeed in life! Set Goals!" We hear these words all the time from parents, teachers, counselors, coaches, and other adults, and I agree, it can get pretty old sometimes to be constantly nagged about something that we don't really want to think about right now. I mean why should we worry SO much about our future, when we have more important things to worry about right now? Like the big game tonight or who we're going to ask to prom! Living in the moment is fun and exciting, so why even think about the future already? But the truth is, when it comes to having goals, the adults are right about this one, and we should pay close attention to what they have to say, and ultimately, take their word for it.

"If you never dream, how can you have a dream come true?"

–Langston Hughes

So what exactly does it mean to have a goal or to set goals for yourself? Goals are a way to plan how to get something you want. They're maps for your future, and baby steps to a life full of accomplishments. That may sound cheesy, but if you really think about it, it makes sense. Goals keep us focused, and when we have goals in life, no matter how big or small they are, it helps us stay on track for creating positive outcomes for ourselves and a successful life. Think of people you look up to, or people you admire who have gone far in life. Would they be anywhere near where they are today without setting goals for themselves? Every successful person has that in common. They figure out what they want, and decide how to make it happen. They set goals.

Goals can come in all shapes and sizes. Some goals are smaller, like your goal to make an A on your next Chemistry test, or to score a goal in your next soccer game, or your goal to actually come home by curfew the next time your parents tell you to. But many goals, especially at our age, are important because like adults love to remind us, the goals we set for ourselves now will change our lives forever! They're right. Short-term and long-term goals are both significant to what we accomplish in life. The short goals are the baby steps to our bigger goals, and together our short-term and long-term goals take us places!! They guide us to get where we want to go.

There is no type of positive goal that isn't worth setting! It's not like goals have to be written down, or typed up. They can be, but they definitely don't have to be! Even if you simply tell yourself over and over that you want to accomplish a certain goal, you're a lot closer to actually reaching it. Realizing what you want and how you're going to get it is one of the most important parts! No matter how small or big the goal is, goals help us realize that we're one step closer to accomplishing something that we set our mind to. Goals are ingredients. When you break your dreams up into

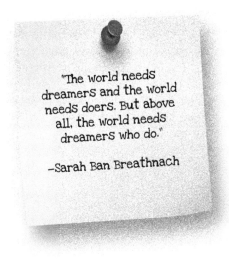

"The world needs dreamers and the world needs doers. But above all, the world needs dreamers who do."

–Sarah Ban Breathnach

goals, you can reach them one by one, knowing that you're accomplishing what you've always wanted to accomplish. This might sound like a weird analogy, but think of your dreams as being your favorite dessert. The goals are the ingredients. They make up the recipe, and when mixed together the right way, you end up with what you want! You reach your dreams.

"Shoot for the moon. Even if you miss, you'll land among the stars."

–Les Brown

By setting goals, you have nothing to lose, just the chance to use your drive and ambition to gain something positive. With a good attitude, setting goals is worth it!! And remember, if for some reason you don't reach a goal on your first try, or even your second, or third, keep trying. I have a poster up in my room with one of my favorite quotes of all time, and it reminds me to persevere. It's by Winston Churchill who said "The most important thing to remember is to NEVER, NEVER, NEVER give up." He's exactly right!

So maybe you're thinking, "I don't have time to set goals! It's just a waste of time, and I don't even know what goals I want to set for myself." Well, my answer to that is simple; everyone has to start somewhere. Setting goals is different for everyone, so let's look at some different ways to set goals…

For some people, goals have to be written down. It makes them seem more realistic, since they're actually there to read. If you think this would be the case for you, then that's what you should do. Take time to brainstorm short-term, mid-term, and long-term goals. Try to put them in order of importance, and decide which goals should come first. Jot them down on scrap paper, or an index card, and keep it somewhere where you can easily find it, like a computer desk drawer, or a wallet.

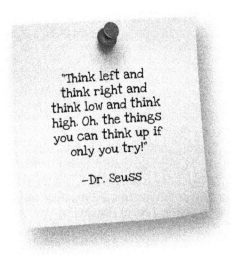

"Think left and think right and think low and think high. Oh, the things you can think up if only you try!"

—Dr. Seuss

Or maybe you're a very visual person like me, and you want to be able to see them easily. If that sounds like you, I'd suggest making a poster or collage of your goals. Start with about 10 or 15 goals, and leave room to add more. You'd be surprised how short a time it takes before you're at 50, or even 100! Design it, decorate it, and hang it somewhere where you'll see it every day.

For some people, goals don't necessarily have to be written down, and that's fine too. Keep mental notes of goals that are important to you, and what you want to accomplish. Goals are goals, whether they're written down or not. And whichever way you choose, the important thing is to set goals, because they lead us to great things.

Visualization is one way to make things happen. It has been proven that when people visualize the things they want in life, and surround themselves with the idea of who they see themselves to be, that they're able to get there much easier! That's why a *wall of goals* is something really cool! And they can look pretty cool too! Some of you may already have walls of goals, and not even know it. Maybe you want to play in the NFL someday, and you have posters of pro football players. By having these posters that you see every day, the idea of you someday being where they are is more likely to come true. With that being said, a wall of goals helps us picture who we want to be, and where we want to go in life. By visualizing, it makes our goals more realistic!

How do we make a wall of goals? Ok, so you don't have to call it a wall of goals, but the point is that you decorate a wall or an area of your room that you'll see each day and it will remind you of your goals. Use magazine clippings, newspaper articles, pictures, postcards, posters, drawings, paintings, quotes, practically anything that has to do with goals and dreams you may have, and add them to that wall or put them in a journal or notebook. After all, seeing is believing, right? And when you believe that you can do something, you're already halfway there!!

Here are some other ideas on how to dream big and make things happen!

✓ Make a list of 100 things you want within your lifetime. They can be small goals, big goals, or a mixture of the two. Don't just list 25 or 50, but really try to choose 100. It's actually a lot of fun to do!

✓ Think BIG! Don't just limit yourself to small goals, or things that you already know you're capable of. Go above and beyond. Remember that the sky is the limit!

✓ Keep a positive attitude about what you want. Don't doubt yourself.

✓ Tell other people about your goals. Talking about them with others will make them more realistic and more likely to come true.

✓ Ignore the haters. Some people get jealous of successful people and try to knock them down. But don't let them. Keep moving forward despite what anyone else thinks.

"It's kind of fun to do the impossible."

—Walt Disney

✓ Take baby steps. Of course it's awesome if you're able to take a huge leap towards your goal, but if you don't have the resources to do that, then just take baby steps. Every single step takes you closer!

✓ Keep your eye on the prize! Remember what it is you wanted in the first place, and remind yourself of how amazing it will feel once you actually reach your goals.

Setting goals helps remind us that we really are here for a reason and that everyone has the potential to do amazing things in life!

Write About It: Dreaming BIG and Setting Goals

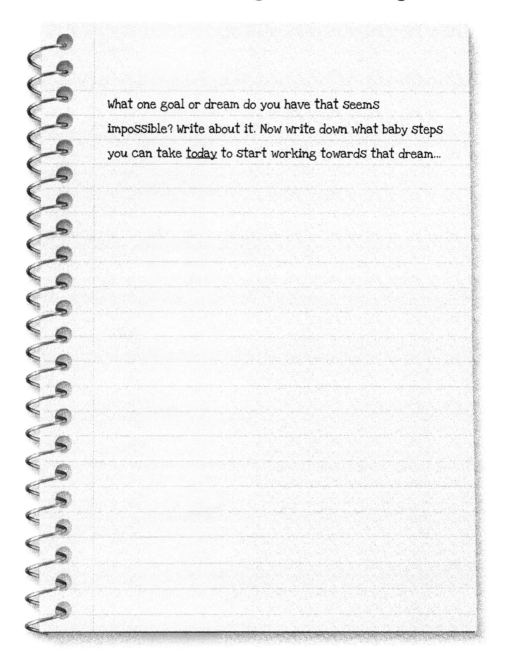

What one goal or dream do you have that seems impossible? Write about it. Now write down what baby steps you can take <u>today</u> to start working towards that dream...

Chapter 12. "Never, Never, Never Give Up!"

Success can be defined in a million different ways. Some people may think of success as being wealthy, some people may think of it as having fame, or some may think of it as reaching a goal or accomplishment. It can have several different meanings, but its meaning is relevant to each person. You may view success completely differently from the people around you, and that's cool. Take a few minutes and think about what success means to you. Close your eyes and imagine your life as it would be if you were as successful as you could possibly dream of. What would your life be like? Put yourself there right now...

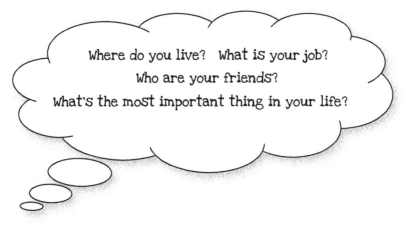

Where do you live? What is your job?

Who are your friends?

What's the most important thing in your life?

If you had the chance to guarantee for yourself that life that you've just pictured, would you do that? Would you try to make it happen? If you did, don't you agree that never giving up would play a huge role in determining whether or not you lived that life of your dreams?

I've always looked up to really successful people. To me, success is all about being happy and content with your life—feeling like you've lived for something and accomplished what you've wanted. If someone is happy with their life, and happy with who they are and where they've taken their life, then you know they're doing something right. I used to sit and wonder how people got to that point—that point of feeling accomplished, and feeling happy and proud. How did they become rockstars, famous actors, founders of organizations, comedians, professional athletes, valedictorians in high school, starting players for the soccer team, first chair in the band competition? I tried to think about what they all had in common, which was hard because success comes in so many different forms. The people I look up to, these successful role models, were all going in different directions. I mean, an Olympic gymnast doesn't take the same steps to reach his or her goal as a lead singer in a famous band, right? One's at the gym, training and working on skills, and the other is writing music or practicing songs. They have different dreams, and accomplish separate things, but there is one thing that every single one of them has in common. They never give up. They never gave up. They probably know how important it is to continue to never give up. Knowing what they wanted, they tried and tried and tried to get to where they wanted to. Am I saying that success came easily to them? No, not at all. They had obstacles and hard situations, and times where they felt like giving up completely. But the simple fact that they kept on going is what separates them from everyone else.

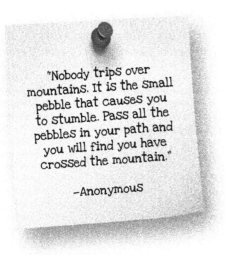

"Nobody trips over mountains. It is the small pebble that causes you to stumble. Pass all the pebbles in your path and you will find you have crossed the mountain."

–Anonymous

Sometimes when we look at famous people, or people who are well known, or people who we consider "successful," we may think, "wow, they're really lucky!" But is it really luck? In some cases, I'm sure it is. Some people end up in the right place at the right time and are given opportunities like no one else. But in most cases, it isn't luck at all. It's hard work, ambition, courage, determination, perseverance…and wow how the list goes on! Sure we can sit around waiting for that lucky opportunity to come our way, but we may end up waiting our entire lives to get somewhere. Or if we're faced with something challenging or scary, we can simply give up, take the easy way out, and call it a day. I can't speak for everyone who's ever accomplished something great in life, but I can say that I'm pretty sure the majority of people who have accomplished great things would agree that never giving up is a huge part of what got them to where they are. That's something they have in common—that they never gave up, and despite obstacles or difficulties, they kept pushing through to get to the top.

Let's check out 14-year-old Whitley's story about never giving up…

I'm on the swim team at school and I'm just a freshman so I'm not exactly in big races or anything. I'm not really a speed demon either haha. A couple of weeks ago, my coach was deciding which races we would be in. She looked at me, smiled, and told me I was doing a 500! 500 meters of swimming is ten laps (a lap is down the pool and back). I honestly was *speechless; literally I was staring at her open-mouthed. After a second I asked her if she was serious and if I was supposed to swim it by myself. Of course the answer to both my questions was "yes." So I began to freak out for the following days before our meet. I trained and worked on my endurance, but I was still in full flip-out mode. On the day of the meet I was pretty much almost hysterical, hyperventilating and all. My event was towards the end so I had plenty of time to freak. Then they called my event. Shaking, I got up on the diving block and adjusted my goggles. I looked up and the WHOLE swim team was at the end of my lane, already cheering me on! So I really started freaking out because I didn't want to let them down. They blew the whistle and I dove in, thankful that my goggles didn't fill up with water. As soon as I came up for air, I heard my teammates cheering so loud that I could even hear them clearly underwater. I thought to myself, "So far, so good." I was on the third lap and keeping a steady pace. Then I got to the fifth lap. I swore I was going to die. The team could tell that I was getting tired, and I was still only halfway done. They started screaming and cheering louder and louder, barely stopping to take a breath. I honestly couldn't believe the support. I mean, I knew then that I had to finish **big** for them. After all, they knew I could do it. And I did. ☺ I finished my 500 in approximately 10 minutes, 36 seconds. That's still a long time, but for my first time, it was pretty awesome! It was seriously a challenge to overcome! Since that day, I've done three more 500s and I have one coming up next week!*

—Whitley, age 14

Whitley was scared at first! The 500-meter race was something she had never done before, and she had a lot of pressure knowing that her whole team was depending on her. But she didn't just say "no" to her coach, or stop and quit halfway through the race. She kept going, and achieved something great because of that. Perseverance can apply to so many different areas of your life! Whether it's working hard for your sports team, or striving to get good grades, or working towards a goal that seems impossible, sticking to it is the answer! You just have to keep at it, and remember that every little bitty step is one more step towards success!

"Wherever you go, go with all your heart"

–Confucius

So although we've heard this our entire life, we've just reestablished how important it is to keep trying, persevere, and never give up. We know that's the right thing to do, but is it much easier said than done? Um, yeah! Of course it is! Giving up is easy, but pushing through is difficult. So how can we remind ourselves to never give up? Well, here are three easy ways.

1. Think of your future

2. Worst case you fall, so just get back up

3. Make it part of who you are

1. Think of your future:

So what do I mean by that? Well, I mean just what I said. Think of your future. Think of what you're working towards and remember what it is you wanted in the first place and why you wanted it. If you remind yourself that all the

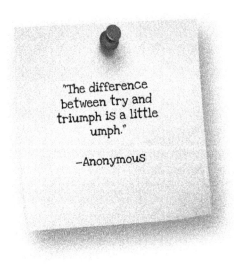

"The difference between try and triumph is a little umph."

−Anonymous

hard work will be worth it in the end, then all that hard work doesn't seem so hard. Sure, you'll have to push yourself and make a lot of effort, but when you have to work hard for something in life, it's that much more important and rewarding when you get there. You'll appreciate things more when you work hard to get them. So if there's ever a time when you're thinking about tossin' out a dream, or letting go of a goal, re-think of why you wanted it in the first place. Because maybe afterall, that dream of yours is way worth the effort. When you show yourself where you're going, and allow yourself to see the destination, getting there isn't so bad.

2. Worst case you fall, so just get back up:

In gymnastics, I learned this "get back up when you fall" lesson the hard way. One day at practice we were working on back-walkovers on the high beam. All the other girls on my team were getting the hang of it. They'd arch backwards into their walkover with perfect hand and foot placement. But it wasn't so easy for me. I got scared. Anything forwards, I was good to go. But I wasn't so excited about this back-walkover. My coach was getting frustrated with me for being scared, and I felt bad for letting her down. She said "Becca, just do it. I'm right here. I'm spotting you. You can do it, don't be afraid." So, trusting her, I arched back and proudly placed my hands on the beam behind me, but while kicking over, I got a nice surprise. My coach pushed me off the beam. Yep...completely knocked me right off the beam. It was so scary! She literally took her hands and shoved me off while I was kicking over. I was so confused! I couldn't believe she would do that to me!

"Our greatest glory is not in never falling, but in rising up every time we fail."

–Confucius

I fell onto the mat next to the beam, and sat there—angry and sore. When I asked her why she pushed me, she calmly responded that she just wanted me to see that it was the worst thing that could happen to me. And she was right. I didn't die, I didn't get hurt (although I easily could've), and it didn't ruin my life. In fact, by being knocked off the beam, it showed me that the worst thing that could happen while trying to do my back-walkover is that I fall off. And if that's the case, I would just have to get back up and try again. At first, I was angry with my coach for letting go when I thought I could trust her—but I have to admit that she had a good point, and it taught me a lot about myself as a gymnast. In life, it's the same way. When we have goals or dreams for ourselves, it's easy to be afraid of failing. That's normal and natural. But we just have to make sure that we don't let that fear get the best of us. We need to remember that yeah, worst case, we may fall down, get knocked down, or completely fail. But that doesn't mean we can't try and try again. When you fall, don't give up—get back up, and you're one **huge** step closer to getting where you want.

3. Make it part of who you are

When I say this, I'm talking about making the whole "never give up" mentality part of who you are. If you always remind yourself to stick out tough situations, and strive to keep going, it'll become a habit for you. Tough situations will become easier because you'll know how to deal with them. When we realize how important it is to never give up, we can accomplish so much more and go further with our goals. Any time you think of giving up, tell yourself you're not a quitter. If you never quit, you'll always get somewhere.

When I started writing this book, I didn't actually think it would turn into what it has. I figured I'd gradually have some paragraphs jotted down in a journal, but I didn't think I'd push myself to come this far—to write a whole book, and deal with the whole publishing process which can be really frustrating and extremely overwhelming. There were so many times when I'd be writing, and I'd say to myself, "what the heck am I doing? Why am I even writing this and working so hard on it?" But I'd have to remind myself about the goal I wanted to reach—the goal of finishing the book, publishing it, and sharing my words with young people. It wasn't about just writing down words, it was about getting out a message to teens and helping teens believe in themselves. That's what pushed me to get through this. (Plus lots of encouragement from my friends and family! Thanks guys! ☺)

"Never underestimate the power of dreams and the influence of the human spirit."

–Wilma Rudolph

I can't tell you how many times I'd throw down my pen and stomp out of my room yelling "Ok mom and dad…I quit! There will be no book. I'm giving up." And I'd try to believe that. The reason was that it was difficult. I had challenges popping up left and right, and on top of having to deal with school and work and drama, sometimes I didn't want to have to deal with writing this book and trying to make it good. And they'd say to me "Well, Bec, it's your decision. Just make sure you don't do something you'll regret." And when they said that, I'd always think to myself, "Will I regret it if I don't write this book?" My answer was always—thankfully—"yes." And I carried on and pushed myself to finish writing. I remembered the goal I set for myself and thought about how it would be worth the hard work in the end. It was just a matter of reminding myself of that. I got knocked down by myself and others. I lacked confidence, and felt like it wasn't good enough. I got comments from other people about how they thought the whole idea was stupid. I doubted myself. But I had to remember what I set out to do in the first place, and I had to remember that nothing worth having comes easily. So although it was hard, I just did it. I wrote, and wrote, and wrote, and never gave up. Looking back, I know that is the only reason this book was completed. The fact that I never let myself give up, even though there were SO many times when I wanted to, is what lead me to the finish line.

It's so easy to want things in life, and think "I'm gonna have that, or I'm gonna do that, or I'm gonna become this." And it's usually pretty easy to take the first step towards reaching that goal. But following through and getting to the end is something entirely different. Perseverance, determination, and hard work—that's the stuff that success is made of. If there is *anything* you want to do in your life, don't be afraid to try. Don't be afraid to do it. Once we start towards a goal, we just have to **keep going**! I promise in the end, you'll feel so great about yourself. When you want to accomplish something, believing you can do it and sticking to it is the most important part of getting there.

"If you never give up, then you never fail. And when you never give up, you discover that one of the best parts about getting where you're trying to go is the beauty and excitement of getting there." This is something I wrote in my journal on April 18, 2008. That was part of the journal entry that sparked the idea for this book. ☺

"The most important thing to remember is to never, never, never give up."

–Winston Churchill

Write About It: "Never, Never, Never Give Up"

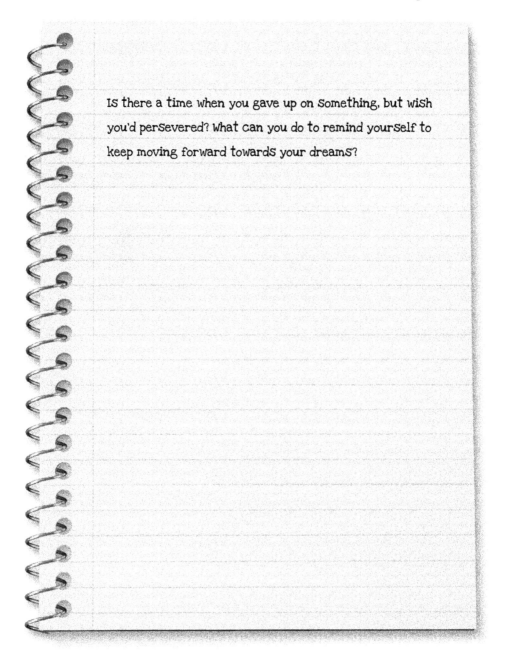

Is there a time when you gave up on something, but wish you'd persevered? What can you do to remind yourself to keep moving forward towards your dreams?

"Every Great Dream Begins With a Dreamer..."

Congratulations! You just finished reading all 12 chapters of this book! What are you going to do next? Go to Disney World!? Just kidding, I know this isn't the Super Bowl. But hopefully you somewhat have a feeling of accomplishment now that you've gotten through the entire book, and I *really* hope you enjoyed it! So what are you thinking right now? Do you feel inspired? Haha. I'm sitting here right now thinking, "Wow! Did I really just finish writing this book?!"

Ever since I was younger, I wasn't exactly what would be considered a great reader. My mind was always going in a million different directions and not a single direction pointed toward the words that were written on the page I was gazing at. It's true—I had some serious comprehension issues haha. Reading just didn't come easily to me...not by any means. But writing sort of did. I enjoyed it so much more, and it was something I understood; something that held my short attention span.

"Sail away from the safe harbor. Catch the trade winds in your sails. Explore. Dream. Discover."

–Mark Twain

That's why looking back now, the whole fact that I wrote this book is a little surprising. I took something I love to do (writing) and ended up creating something that I continue to struggle with (reading books). I know there are so many other young people out there just like me who aren't always excited about picking up a book and reading the whole thing. But I think that's one of the reasons I wanted this book to be different. Actually, I know that's one of the reasons.

I didn't want this book to be boring, difficult to read, or completely pointless. Instead, I wanted you to have the chance to appreciate it for what it is, understand what I was saying, and most importantly, enjoy reading it and learn some things about yourself. I'm not a college graduate with a degree in writing or an expert on how to grow up. (I mean really, who is an expert on growing up?!) But what I *am* is a teenager, who loves writing and helping others. I wrote all of this from the heart—every single word. I didn't talk stuff up, or try to sound all proper. I was just myself. I'm aware that I don't have all the answers, and maybe you didn't agree with everything I said, but regardless of that, there is one thing that I hope you take with you after reading *Live High on Life™*.

A lot of the time at our age we get so caught up in the hustle and bustle, the stress, and the drama, that we forget to stop and really think about who we are and who we've let ourselves become. We see people on TV and think, "Are we supposed to live like that?" Or look at pictures in magazines and on posters and think, "Maybe I'm supposed to look like that." Or we're surrounded by peers and influenced to the point where we might think, "Am I supposed to be just like them?" But the real truth is, we don't have to do any of those things. We don't have to be any certain perfect person. We're not here to be everyone else. We're here to be ourselves, and no one more or less than that.

"Be yourself. Who else is better qualified?" That's a quote by Frank J. Giblin that I've had posted on my wall since I was in middle school. Sometimes I wish I followed that advice more than I actually did, but I can learn from that. But the quote makes sense, don't you think? There's only one you in the world, and no one is going to fit that role better than you will. So that gives

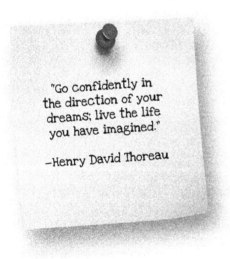

"Go confidently in the direction of your dreams; live the life you have imagined."

–Henry David Thoreau

you the opportunity to live up to who you want to be. If there's something you don't like about yourself that can be changed, change it. If there's something you know you can improve, improve it. If there's something you've always wanted to do, go and do it!!! We won't get anywhere in life by sitting on the sidelines. Just like I said in the beginning of the book and all throughout, your life is only as good as you make it. You have the power to do just that—make it what you want it to be.

When we love ourselves, keep a good attitude, open our hearts to other people and the world around us, and strive to be the best we can be every day, then we win. It's as simple as that, but I know it's definitely not always easy to change. No one wants to sit down and think, "whoa, I guess I could've done this differently, or reacted a little better to that, or been nicer to them…" We don't want to think that we do things wrong. We don't want to list mistakes or flaws. I know I don't. Changing and improving our lives takes time, and a lot of effort, but after a while, it'll come naturally. The principles of this book and the *Live High on Life*™ style can change your world. By living this lifestyle, we're creating for ourselves the life that **we** want!

We won't just wake up one morning and decide, "Okay, this is who I am. I figured out who I am!" Instead, we have the ability to change and grow and learn and it's an amazing thing. We're lucky we can do that. So don't ever settle for less than what you want or how you want to live. Follow your dreams, set high standards for yourself, and NEVER lose sight of who you are. Because you're capable of accomplishing incredible things! You just have to remember that and remind yourself. I can't tell you how many times I doubted myself when writing this book. But I had to believe in myself, and believe that I was able to do something great. There are times every single day that we're unsure of our capabilities, but we're a whole lot stronger than we can imagine, and we can accomplish way more than we think.

We're here to make THIS life what WE want to make it, with our own opinions, decisions, morals, and personalities. We may be young, but we still want what everyone wants in life—to be happy. When you build your life up each and every day and try to improve who you are, you'll feel good. You'll feel soooo good! You'll find that happiness that everyone wants to feel. Life is much more fulfilling when you take control and make it what you want it to be. So do just that, and become the greatest person you can be. These are **your** teenage years, so make the most of them!

Thanks so much for reading my book. I wish you all the happiness and success you can possibly imagine.

"Every great dream begins with a dreamer. Always remember you have within you the strength, the patience, and the passion to reach for the stars and change the world."

—Harriet Tubman

Live High on Life™ every single moment.

With peace and love,
Becca ♡

Thank-Yous

This book would not have been possible without all the incredible love, inspiration, support, and guidance I received along the way.

Thanks to my dad, Ken, for always believing in me and allowing me to believe in myself. You knew that this book could be a reality from the very beginning and encouraged me to keep moving towards my goal! Thank you, Debbie, my amazing mom, for your unconditional love and support. You never let me doubt myself, and you have been such an inspiration to me throughout all of this. Thank you, Andrew and Kyle, my awesome brothers, for standing by me and encouraging me.

Thank you, Kate Whitfield, my empowering mentor, for showing me that it is totally possible to reach my goals!

Thank you so much, Ernie Wertheim, my wonderful uncle, for creating the beautiful cover and the awesome interior design. You took my vision and turned it into something cooler than I could've imagined. This book would not be what it is without you! Thanks to everyone at Outskirts Press who helped make this book possible.

Thanks to my grandfather, Alfred Wertheim, for all your help throughout the editing process. Thank you Pam Musinski, my amazing aunt, for sparking this vision inside me and thank you Bill Musinski, my uncle, for always checking up on my progress and showing that you cared.

Thank you, Tyler Trent, my best friend and boyfriend, for constantly supporting me and believing in me. When I wanted to give up, you encouraged me to keep chasing this dream.

Thanks to my great friends, Jordan Kelly, Rachel Trent, Blake Everhart, and Katie Engle, for your feedback, opinions, support, and motivation.

Thank you, Mrs. Anne Ellison, my 4th grade teacher, for allowing me to see something great in myself. Thank you to all the teachers and staff at Charles D. Owen High School for inspiring me to do amazing things with my life.

A very special thanks to all the teens who contributed to this book: John Bass, Maddi Bontrager, Whitley Burleson, Peyton Byrd, Katie Fiore, Shae Frizsell, Devin Gaynor, Kristianna George, Adam Greenspan, Emily-Anne Rigal, Ellie Shown, Kyle Travers, Olivia Tyson, and Hillary Webb. I am so grateful that your inspirational words could be part of it!

Thank you all for constantly encouraging me to follow this dream and make it a reality. I am truly blessed to have such incredible friends and family in my life.

Inspiring Books and Awesome People

Check out These Inspiring Books!

- *The 7 Habits of Highly Effective Teens* by Sean Covey

- *The 6 Most Important Decisions You'll Ever Make* by Sean Covey

- *SUCCESS for Teens* by the Editors of the SUCCESS Foundation

- *The Success Principles for Teens* by Jack Canfield and Kent Healy

- *Chicken Soup for the Soul®* book series, created by Jack Canfield and Mark Victor Hansen

- *Oh, The Places You'll Go* by Dr.Seuss (My fav!)

- Ladies, check out *The Empowered Gal's 9 Life Lessons* by Kate Whitfield

Both guys and gals, follow these cool people on Twitter!

- **@S4Teens** (SUCCESS for Teens™)

- **@dosomething** (www.dosomething.org)

- **@freedomwriters**

- **@WeStopHate** (www.youtube.com/westophate and westophate.org)

- **@Schmiddlebopper** (Emily-Anne Rigal, an incredible "teen-esteem" expert and founder of WeStopHate. Visit www.youtube.com/schmiddlebopper)

Gals, follow these amazing women on Twitter for daily doses of inspiration!

- **@KateWhitfield** (Author of *The Empowered Gal's 9 Life Lessons* and the founder of Empowered Gal, Inc.! Visit www.empoweredgal.com)

- **@annshoket** (She's the editor of *Seventeen!* Be sure to follow **@seventeenmag**)

- **@DeborahReber** (Author and advocate for teen girls. Check out her awesome blog at www.smartgirlsknow.com)

110

· **@JessWeiner** (Creator of an incredible group of women called Actionists®. Visit www.jessweiner.com to check out her blog, and find out how *you* can become a more confident girl.)

Contact Me!

I would seriously love to hear from you! Questions, comments, suggestions, anything…Don't be a stranger! ☺

Visit the website... www.livehighonlife.com

Email me .... Becca@livehighonlife.com

Follow me on Twitter........................@BeccaWertheim and @livehighonlife

Check out my blog................................ www.BeccaWertheim.blogspot.com

Become a fan on Facebook...................... www.facebook.com/livehighonlife

Resources for You

Volunteer Opportunities

- www.ymca.net/be-involved (I work at the YMCA and I **love** it ☺)

- www.dosomething.org (Apply to be a member of their Youth Advisory Council)

- www.volunteermatch.org

- www.disney.com/friendsforchange

Protecting & Respecting our Environment

- Wanna check out something *really* cool? Calculate your ecological footprint at www.footprintnetwork.org/en/index.php/GFN/page/calculators/ and get awesome tips on how *you* can make a difference right away!

- www.epa.gov/waste/education/teens/

- Visit as many National Parks as you can! Some of my favorites include:

  The Blue Ridge Parkway in North Carolina and Virginia, Great Smoky Mountains National Park in North Carolina and Tennessee, Grand Tetons National Park in Wyoming, Yosemite National Park in California, Zion National Park in Utah, Grand Canyon National Park in Arizona, Cumberland Island National Seashore in Georgia, and Yellowstone National Park in Wyoming, Montana, and Idaho. Visit www.nps.gov for more info!

- Help make a difference in our world! Visit www.disney.com/friendsforchange for ideas!

Empowering Websites

- www.SUCCESSfoundation.org "Inspiring Tomorrow's Achievers"

- www.seancovey.com/teens.html

Suicide Prevention & Information

- www.suicidepreventionlifeline.org or call 1-800-273-TALK (8255)

- 1-800-SUICIDE (784-2433)

- American Foundation for Suicide Prevention, www.afsp.org

Bullying and Cyberbullying Prevention and Information

- www.teensagainstbullying.org with spokesperson Demi Lovato

- www.stopcyberbullying.org

Abuse Helplines and Information

- Sexual Assault—Visit www.rainn.org or call 1-800-656-HOPE (4673)

- Love Is Respect: National Teen Dating Abuse Helpline—Chat with someone live on their website at www.loveisrespect.org, or call 1-866-331-9474

- National Domestic Violence Hotline: Visit www.ndvh.org or call

  1-800-799-SAFE (7233)

Eating Disorder Helpline & Information

- www.nationaleatingdisorders.org or call 1-800-931-2237

- http://kidshealth.org/teen

Self-Esteem & Self-Worth Information

- http://kidshealth.org/teen/your_mind/body_image/body_image.html

- www.seventeen.com/health/tips/body-peace-nplp-0508

- http://teenadvice.about.com/od/selfesteem/Confidence_SelfEsteem.htm

Healthy Choices & Nutrition Information

- www.MyPyramid.gov

- www.fitness.gov

- http://kidshealth.org/teen

- http://win.niddk.nih.gov/publications/take_charge.htm

Substance Abuse Facts & Information

- www.AboveTheInfluence.com

- www.teencentral.net/

- www.sadd.org

- www.drugfree.org

- http://checkyourself.com

- Center for Substance Abuse and Mental Health Services Referral Line: 1-800-662-4357

- Is someone in your life an alcoholic? Want help on how to deal with it? Visit www.al-anon.alateen.org/alateen.html

Sex Facts & Information

- www.stayteen.org

- www.itsyoursexlife.com

- www.sexetc.org

Bibliography

Chapter 2, It's All About Attitude:

Barefoot's World.
The Wolves Within. www.barefootsworld.net/wolveswithin.html.

Chapter 4, Creating Great Character:

Rohn, Jim.
Forging Your Character, an excerpt from *Leading an Inspired Life.* www.jimrohn.com/index.php?main_page=page&id=1251&utm_source=jrn-4_26_&utm_medium=email&utm_campaign=ezines.

As a world-renowned author and success expert, Jim Rohn touched millions of lives during his 46-year career as a motivational speaker and messenger of positive life change.

For more information on Jim and his popular personal achievement resources or to subscribe to the weekly Jim Rohn Newsletter, visit www.JimRohn.com.

Chapter 9, It's Your Body:

United Stated Department of Agriculture.
www.MyPyramid.gov. Public Domain.

CPSIA information can be obtained
at www.ICGtesting.com
Printed in the USA
LVHW02s0311111217
559363LV00036B/2920/P